CITYSPOTS
GRANA

CW00327834

WHAT'S IN YOUR GUIDEBOOK?

Independent authors Impartial up-to-date information from our travel experts who meticulously source local knowledge.

Experience Thomas Cook's 165 years in the travel industry and guidebook publishing enriches every word with expertise you can trust.

Travel know-how Contributions by thousands of staff around the globe, each one living and breathing travel.

Editors Travel-publishing professionals, pulling everything together to craft a perfect blend of words, pictures, maps and design.

You, the traveller We deliver a practical, no-nonsense approach to information, geared to how you really use it.

CITYSPOTS
GRANADA

Nick Inman

Written by Nick Inman
Original photography by Nick Inman
Front cover photography (Palacio de Comares, Alhambra) © Giovanni Simeone/
www.4cornersimages.com
Series design based on an original concept by Studio 183 Limited

Produced by Cambridge Publishing Management Limited
Project Editor: Amanda Learmonth
Layout: Trevor Double
Maps: PC Graphics
Transport map: © Communicarta Limited

Published by Thomas Cook Publishing
A division of Thomas Cook Tour Operations Limited
Company Registration No. 1450464 England
PO Box 227, Unit 18, Coningsby Road
Peterborough PE3 8SB, United Kingdom
email: books@thomascook.com
www.thomascookpublishing.com
+ 44 (0) 1733 416477
ISBN: 978-1-84157-774-6

First edition © 2007 Thomas Cook Publishing
Text © 2007 Thomas Cook Publishing
Maps © 2007 Thomas Cook Publishing
Series/Project Editor: Kelly Anne Pipes
Production/DTP: Steven Collins

Printed and bound in Spain by GraphyCems

CONTENTS

SYMBOLS KEY

The following symbols are used throughout this book:

ⓐ address ⓣ telephone ⓦ website address
ⓛ opening times ⓝ public transport connections ⓘ important

The following symbols are used on the maps:

𝒊 information office   O city
✈ airport   O large town
✚ hospital   o small town
𝔙 police station   = motorway
🚏 bus station   — main road
🚆 railway station   — minor road
✝ cathedral   — railway
❶ numbers denote featured cafés & restaurants

Hotels and restaurants are graded by approximate price
as follows:

£ budget   ££ mid-range   £££ expensive

◐ *The spectacular setting of the Alhambra*

INTRODUCING
Granada

Introduction

'Granada: the land I've dreamed of...' run the words of a famous song and indeed this southern Spanish city is and always has been the stuff of people's dreams. Situated at the foot of the highest mountain range in the Iberian peninsula, the Sierra Nevada ('Snowy Mountains'), which form a constant backdrop, Granada is most visited for its Moorish heritage: the exotic art and architecture of medieval Europe's great Muslim civilisation. No one comes to Granada without seeing, in particular, the incomparable fortress-palace of the Alhambra, which is almost overwhelming in the magnificence of its interior decoration, making it a strong contender to be one of the new Seven Wonders of the World.

Below the Alhambra is a busy city of a quarter of a million people. A sizeable percentage of the population is made up of university students and other young people, and this happy age-imbalance has encouraged a convivial, easy-going bar-hopping culture that is another of Granada's key attractions. Most bars in the city lay on a complementary *tapa* (snack) with each drink you order and serendipitously eating your way around the city in the company of friends can easily get addictive.

Another great thing about Granada is its compactness. It is a smallish city that positively encourages you to explore on foot. There is virtually no monument, museum, shop or bar of significance that you have to take public transport to get to – although it's always an option.

Being small makes Granada easy to get into and just as easy to get out of. A short series of hairpin bends south takes you up to Europe's southernmost ski station. Alternatively, the Mediterranean beaches of the so-called 'Tropical Coast' are less than an hour away. Between mountain tops and the seashore are the verdant valleys of the Alpujarras, which make good country for hiking or simply chilling out.

● *Plaza Santa Ana, one of the city's many pleasant squares*

When to go

SEASONS & CLIMATE

Granada has an essentially continental climate with strong contrasts between seasons, which are heavily influenced by its altitude (685 m/2,250 ft). The average annual temperature is a cool 14.8°C (58.6°F). January has a typical temperature of 6°C (43°F) with daytime temperatures sometimes as high as 20°C (70°F). August has a typical temperature of 25°C (77°F) but it can climb to a stifling 40°C (100°F). July and August are peak tourist months but they can be unbearably hot. Many local people choose to decamp for the height of the summer. Autumn is a short season but a good time to visit if you are prepared to risk some rain. Almost all the year's rain falls between October and May.

Winters can be cold but also sunny – you'll need heating to sit still in a room but the sun, when it shines, is warm enough to have a coffee out of doors on most days of the year.

Spring comes early, this being southern Spain, and, although there may be bad weather still ahead, the weeks from late March to early June can usually be counted on for mild weather to go with a prodigious growth of flowers in parks and gardens before the heat of the summer takes hold.

ANNUAL EVENTS

There are three traditional fiestas especially worth seeing in Granada: Easter Week, the Crosses of May and the Corpus Christi fair. The ceremony to commemorate the conquest of Granada is also interesting. Any fiesta means free

◔ *Gypsy culture forms an integral part of Granadino life*

entertainment, but don't expect a quiet night's sleep or an easy day's sightseeing. Streets may be blocked off to allow processions to pass; some monuments may be closed; and bars and restaurants are likely to be overflowing with customers.

January
Fiesta de la Toma (Commemoration of the Conquest of Granada)
To celebrate the handing over of the Alhambra by its Muslim rulers to the Christians, a civic-religious ceremony is held with a procession from the Capilla Real to the town hall. Here, the youngest member of the city council theatrically waves the banner of the victorious kingdom of Castile.

March/April
Semana Santa (Easter Week)
Every city in Spain holds processions for Easter Week but no other city can provide a backdrop for the lines of hooded penitents to beat the floodlit silhouette of the Alhambra. There are processions from Palm Sunday to Easter Sunday. Each one takes its own route – those to the Albaicín and Sacromonte are particularly worth seeing – but they are all funnelled into the official route at the end, which goes down Calle Navas, Plaza del Carmen, Calle Reyes Católicos, Calle Mesones, Calle Marquéz de Gerona, Plaza de las Pasiegas and ends at the cathedral. On Thursday night there is an eerily silent procession to the sound of a mournful drum beat.

May/June
Cruces de Mayo (Crosses of May)
Each neighbourhood of the city makes a decorative outdoor cross-cum-altar for itself on this day. The best ones are to be seen in the Albaicín and Realejo. Although there is a competition to choose the best cross, mostly this fiesta is an occasion to fill the streets with life for a day, to sing songs, and to eat broad beans and drink the local Costa wine.

Corpus Christi
For the week around Corpus Christi the city heads out to a purpose-built fairground that throbs to the sound of Sevillana music – a kind of flamenco pop. Well-to-do men dress in their best riding gear and saunter up and down on horseback while women in typical Andalucían flamenco dresses ride in carriages.

PUBLIC HOLIDAYS
Año Nuevo (New Year's Day) 1 Jan
Día de Reyes (Epiphany) 6 Jan
Andalucía Day 28 Feb
Jueves Santo (Maundy Thursday) Mar/Apr
Viernes Santo (Good Friday) Mar/Apr
Día del Trabajo (Labour Day) 1 May
Asunción de la Virgen (Day of the Assumption) 15 Aug
Día de la Hispanidad (Spain's national day) 12 Oct
Todos Los Santos (All Saints' Day) 1 Nov
Día de la Constitución (Constitution Day) 6 Dec
La Inmaculada Concepción (Immaculate Conception) 8 Dec
Día de Navidad (Christmas Day) 25 Dec

The legacy of the Moors

You can't move in Granada without being reminded that for 750 years the city was under the dominion of the Moors – the Islamic civilisation of southern Spain more properly known as Al Andalus. Granada was the last bastion of the last Muslim kingdom in Europe, and it is impossible to understand the city, its history, its architecture or its traditions without fully appreciating the lingering impact of this.

Yet Granada hasn't always been proud of its past. In the wake of the Reconquest, mosques were converted into churches as fast as humanly possible; castles and palaces – including the Alhambra – were treated to 'Christian' makeovers; and the rambling, inscrutable oriental street pattern of much of the city centre was straightened out according to Renaissance fashion leaving only the Albaicín in its original state.

But there was no getting away from the legacy of the Moors. The map of Spain is sprinkled with Arabic place names and the Spanish language would be much poorer without the many words derived from Arabic. Moorish craft traditions still flourish. In the countryside, crops introduced by the Moors are still grown, watered by the same ingenious irrigation systems in use 600 or more years ago.

Today, all things Moorish are back in fashion and every last lingering trace of Al Andalus is treated as a source of pride. The Alhambra might be the most stunning reminder of the civilisation that once was but you can explore the vanished world of Muslim Spain throughout Andalucía by following a series of routes laid out by an organisation based in Granada's

THE LEGACY OF THE MOORS

Corral del Carbón, the Legado Andalusi (Legacy of Al Andalus)
(🅰 Plaza Isabel la Católica 1–5 ☎ 958 225 995
🆆 www.legadoandalusi.andalucia.es). Leaflets explaining each
route are available (free) from Granada's tourist offices.

🔺 *Exquisite Moorish artistry is best seen at the Alhambra*

History

There was probably a prehistoric settlement on the site of modern Granada before the Romans built the town of Iliberis in the 1st century AD. In the 5th century, on the break-up of the Roman Empire, it came under Visigoth rule.

When, in 711, armies from North Africa overran the Iberian peninsula, Granada, then known as Elvira, soon fell into their hands. But it was still a place of little significance, overshadowed by neighbouring Córdoba, the capital of the caliphate which ruled over Muslim Spain or Al Andalus.

Internal divisions led to the fall of the caliphate in the 11th century, and it broke up into small kingdoms. One of these grew up with the city of Granada as its hub. By now the kings of northern Spain had begun the Reconquest of the south in the name of Christianity; but Granada was destined to be the last bit of territory to defy them.

Muhammad ibn Nasr, the first of the Nasrid dynasty, expanded the borders of Granada to stretch across southern Spain from the Atlantic coast to Almería. Under his rule work began on the magnificent palace-fortress of the Alhambra, the finest achievement of art and architecture produced by the Islamic civilisation of Spain.

Cut off from the rest of the Muslim world, the kingdom of Granada survived until the 15th century when King Fernando of Aragon and Queen Isabel of Castile, the so-called Reyes Católicos (Catholic Monarchs), decided to force its rendition. The fall of Granada on 2 January 1492 brought the unification of Spain, but it was also the start of a long period of decline for the city as attention shifted to Seville and the newly founded capital of Madrid.

Only in the 19th century was Granada 'rediscovered' by foreign travellers, particularly the American writer Washington Irving (see page 64). The Alhambra, which until this time had been wilfully neglected as the embarrassing reminder of heathen times, was at last treated as part of the national heritage.

But Spain was living through turbulent times as regimes came and went. The Spanish Civil War broke out in July 1936 and the city was taken by the rebels under General Franco. Spain emerged from the war in 1939 and endured dictatorship until Franco's death in 1975.

The ensuing transition to democracy brought decentralisation and modernisation, and Granada is now the capital city of one of the eight provinces that make up the region of Andalucía.

● *Plaque displaying the Catholic Monarchs and Christopher Columbus*

Lifestyle

Southern Spain lives at a different pace to much of the rest of Europe and you'd be wise to fit in with it. The day in Granada begins slowly and the morning is long. Lunchtime is late by the standards of most visitors: only tourist-orientated restaurants start serving before 14.00 and it is not unusual to sit down to a full meal after 15.00. A long digestive break follows with or without a siesta, according to personal preference and the time of year. In the summer it makes sense to take a nap in the heat of the day so as to be refreshed and ready to go out when the temperature gets bearable again in the evening. The afternoon only begins at 16.00–17.00 and many people still have half a working day ahead of them before clocking off at 21.00 or so. Dinner is at 22.00 or even 23.00 but is not as heavy as lunch. The long gaps between meals are often filled with mini-meals in a bar or café: a late breakfast at around 11.00; *merienda* (something generally sweet) at 18.00 or 19.00; and tapas at any time the fancy takes.

Granadinos in general – there are exceptions – pride themselves on having a more relaxed attitude to time than people in larger cities. They leave room in life for spontaneity and the unplanned, often at the expense of punctuality. If two friends arrange to meet in a bar, for example, neither will be surprised if the other is an hour or so late, having met up with other friends on the way and stopped to have a drink with them out of courtesy.

Less attractively, Granadinos have a reputation for being brusque, at times to the point of rudeness, but most people you will meet will only be too pleased to help you find your way or buy what you want in a shop.

Particularly important in this gregarious country is to show respect for other people. Always say hello when you enter a shop, bar or any other public place: '*buenos días*' during the day and '*buenas tardes*' (good afternoon/evening) from about 19.00 or 20.00 on, and '*adios*' when you leave.

🔺 *Whiling away the afternoon in a city bar*

Culture

Some locals grumble that Granada is a parochial backwater when it comes to the arts, but it is unfair to compare it with larger cities such as Madrid and Barcelona, or even Seville, and if you arrive without preconceptions you'll probably be agreeably surprised. The city has many good exhibition spaces – several of them in historic buildings – and its music, theatre and dance venues receive their share of international acts on tour.

Granada's two most famous creator-sons are the classical composer Manuel de Falla (1876–1946) and his friend the poet Federico García Lorca, whose early and violent death (see box, page 22) has only enhanced his reputation. Falla wasn't born in Granada but he lived here from 1921 to 1939 and the city's main concert hall is named after him. Two of his best-loved pieces are *Nights in the Gardens of Spain* and *The Three-Cornered Hat*.

Lorca was a great admirer of gypsy culture and he'd be delighted to know that contemporary and traditional flamenco music and dance (not to be confused with the shows for tourists, see page 98) are now being taken seriously by audiences and critics.

There's plenty of homegrown contemporary art too, this being the kind of place that inspires creative types. And look out especially for exhibitions of the art (and science) of an earlier era, Muslim Spain – an area in which Granada inevitably beats other cities hands down.

⬥ One of the cuevas *(caves)* in which flamenco is performed

THE MURDER OF LORCA

At dawn on 19 August 1936, during the early days of the Civil War, one of Spain's greatest poets and playwrights was abducted from a friend's house in Granada and shot by rightwing militiamen in circumstances that have never been fully explained. Federico García Lorca came from a good family and, although he had leftwing leanings, he was not overtly political. He was, however, libertarian and a homosexual – just the sort of person who wouldn't fit into the authoritarian, ultra-Catholic country that Franco and his cronies were planning to turn Spain into. Granada had fallen into the rebel military's hands at the start of the war and it was probably only a matter of time before Lorca was rounded up as an example to other sensitive nonconformists.

Still, in his 37 years of life, Lorca made a reputation for himself, which has endured and made him a secular, literary saint today. He was heavily influenced by the gypsy culture of Andalucía and a champion of the socially disenfranchised, and of women. His best-known plays include *Blood Wedding*, *Yerma* and *The House of Bernarda Alba*.

His birthplace in the town of Fuente Vaqueros (15 km/9 miles northwest of Granada) can be visited, as can his house in Granada, the Huerta de San Vicente (see page 80), which has been turned into a museum.

● *Flamenco dresses for sale*

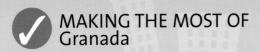

Shopping

The main shopping district of Granada is a rectangle formed by the Gran Vía de Colón, Calle Reyes Católicos, Calle Alhóndiga and Plaza Trinidad but you can continue shopping down Calle de Recogidas and in the streets between Puerta Real and El Realejo. The narrow streets and squares here are either pedestrianised or almost traffic-free, making it easy to move about, although there are often crowds of shoppers and bar-hoppers to contend with.

Some shops – particularly in the Alcaicería (in the centre, see page 84) and on the Cuesta de Gomérez leading up the Alhambra – cater exclusively for tourists and it's rare to find authentic craft goods in such places. If you want a high-quality souvenir from Granada, you should choose a serious, specialised craft shop and be prepared to pay for good workmanship.

Like everywhere else in Europe, it seems, there is a trend towards out-of-town shopping in vast complexes of brand outlets grouped around a hypermarket. You might find a loss-leading bargain in such places but you are unlikely to find

WHAT TO BUY

Pottery is Granada's trademark craft. Guitars are also made in the city. Another good idea for a souvenir is something edible from a delicatessen, such as a bottle of extra virgin olive oil or some ham cured in the mountain air of Trevélez (see page 121).

anything authentically local for sale. Far better is to favour the many small, independent shops that the centre of Granada is still blessed with. Prices are not always higher than in shopping centres – that is a myth – but it is difficult to browse undisturbed and you will be forced to practise your Spanish to get what you want.

⬧ Look out for small, specialised craft shops

El Corte Inglés

Spain's own department store chain is a place to find almost anything you are looking for, including fashion, books and newspapers in English, maps and CDs of Spanish music. The supermarket is a cut above the average with ranges of exquisite gourmet foods. There are branches at Carrera del Genil 20–22 (☎ 958 223 240) and at Arabial 95 and 97 (☎ 958 223 240).

USEFUL SHOPPING PHRASES

What time do the shops open/close?
¿A qué hora abren/cierran las tiendas?
¿A kay ora abren/theeyerran las teeyendas?

How much is this?
¿Cuánto es?
¿Cwantoe es?

Can I try this on?
¿Puedo probarme esto?
¿Pwedo probarme esto?

My size is ...
Mi número es el ...
Mee noomero es el ...

I'll take this one.
Me llevo éste.
Meh yevo esteh.

This is too large/too small/too expensive.
Do you have any others?
Es muy grande/muy pequeño/muy caro. ¿Tienen más?
Es mooy grandeh/mooy pekenio/mooy karo. ¿Teeyenen mas?

Eating & drinking

Installing yourself in a succession of bars, cafés and restaurants is one of the delights of a visit to Granada. The city has a wide choice of places to eat and drink from the old-fashioned and quaint to the vibrantly modern.

For the most part the cuisine is 'typically Andalucían', which means straightforward meat, fish, seafood and vegetable dishes prepared and served with the minimum of complication and formality. With such an abundance of good fresh ingredients to hand there's no need to disguise them with rich sauces. As this is southern Spain, most dishes have olive oil lurking in them somewhere and dairy foods are used minimally.

The main meal in Spain is in the middle of the day and this is when most restaurants offer a cheaper menu, *menu del día*, which typically consists of three courses with a bottle of the house wine included. This is certainly the best way to fill up without spending a lot of money.

RESTAURANT PRICE CATEGORIES

Average price for a three-course meal (*menu del día* if there is one) for one person, excluding drinks, but including tax:

£ = up to €20   ££ = €20–40   £££ = more than €40

Ratings for cafés and bars are:

£ = inexpensive   ££ = moderately priced   £££ = expensive

When looking for a restaurant the best advice is to eat where the locals eat and avoid anywhere that displays photographs of its dishes outside. If in doubt, follow a group of hungry students who will know where to make their money go furthest.

Spain's main failing is its dessert menu, which all too often reduces to a piece of fresh fruit, a scoop of ice cream or the ubiquitous *flan* – crème caramel. But it makes up for this deficiency by being strong on sweet snacks. Granada has several excellent cake shops, *pastelerías*, offering a choice of something to go with a coffee or to fill the long gap between lunch and dinner.

Another weak point for many visitors is breakfast. Only a few bars open early to serve their customers coffee and toast – the

⬤ *Dishes of the day*

local style is to eat it drizzled with olive oil and smeared with tomato rather than spread with butter and jam.

A popular breakfast or midnight snack during fiestas is a portion of *churros* – deep-fried sticks of batter that are sprinkled with sugar and dunked into a cup of coffee or hot chocolate.

Tapas

Where Granada excels is in its tapas bars. Even posh restaurants are likely to have a bar attached where you can eat well without having to order a full meal or eat formally. By tradition, a tapa is served free with each drink in Granada – it will arrive in front of you after a couple of minutes' delay. Most bars serve tapas in a set order so you get something different with each round of drinks. What you get is a matter of luck or knowing the bar. A tapa can be as simple as a saucer of olives or crisps; or it might be a slice of *jamón serrano* or wedge of cured sheep's cheese but it might just as well be something more substantial such as a selection of fried fish, a seafood salad or a portion of paella.

If you want a larger portion ask for a *ración*. But take care: tapas and *raciones* can easily add up to more than a full menu in a restaurant.

The big thing about tapas is that they are available any time of day or night: you'll never hear anyone in Granada tell you the kitchen is closed and there's nothing to eat.

Incidentally, tapas are often a godsend to vegetarians visiting Spain. If nothing else, almost every bar can offer up a *ración* of meat-free salad or a slice of the old stand-by *tortilla de patata* (potato omelette).

USEFUL DINING PHRASES

I would like a table for ... people.
Quisiera una mesa para ... personas.
Keyseeyera oona mesa para ... personas.

May I have the bill, please?
¿Podría traerme la cuenta
por favor?
*¿Pordreea trayerme la cwenta
por fabor?*

Waiter/waitress!
¡Camarero/Camarera!
¡Camareroe/Camarera!

Could I have it well cooked/medium/rare please?
¿Por favor, la carne bien cocida/al punto/roja?
¿Por fabor, la kahrrne beeyen kotheeda/al poontoh/roha?

I am a vegetarian. Does this contain meat?
Soy vegetariano. ¿Tiene carne este plato?
Soy begetahreeahnoh. ¿Teeyene carneh esteh plahtoh?

Where is the toilet (restroom) please?
¿Dónde están los servicios, por favor?
¿Donde estan los serbeetheeos, por fabor?

I would like a cup of/two cups of/another coffee/tea.
Quisiera una taza de/dos tazas de/otra taza de café/té.
*Keyseeyera oona tatha dey/dos tathas dey/otra tatha dey
kafey/tey.*

Entertainment & nightlife

Granada offers a generous choice of entertainment from low- to high-brow, depending on your taste. Largely because of the climate, but also because of the pattern of the working day, nights out begin late and go on later, especially in summer when daytime temperatures are too hot to do anything except cower indoors. During fiestas (see pages 10–12) there will be enough going on in the streets and you won't need to look for amusements elsewhere. The most popular entertainment for foreign visitors to the city is flamenco music and dance (see page 98).

Information & booking

For details of what's on in Granada during your stay, ask at the local tourist office where you'll be able to pick up a free guide to events. Or see the following websites:

ⓦ www.pocketguia.es

ⓦ www.granada.latnetro.com

Two online agencies specialising in booking tickets for entertainment in Spain are:

ⓦ www.entradas.com ⓣ 902 221 622

ⓦ www.servicaixa.com ⓣ 902 332 211

Cinema in English

Most foreign films screened in Spain are dubbed into Spanish. Not many original-version (VO – for *versión original*) English and American films are shown in Granada and your best bet to see one is the university's film club (**Cineclub Universitario**

ⓐ Facultad de Ciencias ☎ 958 243 484) or language school
(**Centro de Lenguas Modernas** ⓐ Placeta del Hospicio Viejo
☎ 958 215 660).

Theatre & concerts

Granada's main theatre is **Teatro Isabel la Católica** (ⓐ Acera del
Casino ☎ 958 222 907), and performances are all in Spanish.
Perhaps more interesting to the visitor is the **Centro Cultural**

⬥ A teterìa (tea shop) is an atmospheric place for a drink or two

Manuel de Falla (☎ 958 222 907 ⓦ www.manueldefalla.org),
which puts on a programme of classical music and dance by
visiting companies.

Nightlife

There are two shifts of nightlife in Granada. If you prefer an
early bed you can happily do the rounds of tapas bars until
23.00 or so. It's only then that serious night people go out to
start their evening in a *bar de copas* – a bar made for drinking
(shorts mainly) with few or no chairs and low light levels. Most
such bars pride themselves on the attractiveness of their
counter staff and their select taste in music. A few have DJs and
dance floors or put on live acts, and some charge admission
accordingly. Only after 24.00 or later do people move on to clubs
(*discotecas*), which may stay open until 06.00 or later. Nightlife
areas shift with the times but the Carrera del Darro and Campo
del Príncipe are good places to start out.

Arts festivals
Festival Internacional de Tango (International Tango Festival)
March. A new creation that has so far proved successful.
☎ 958 271 272 ⓦ www.eltango.com/granada/
EntradaGranada.htm

**Festival Internacional de Música y Danza (International Festival
of Music and Dance)** Last two weeks of June and the first week
of July. Over 50 years old and still going strong, this festival uses
the Alhambra and Generalife among its venues. ☎ 958 221 844
ⓦ www.granadafestival.org

Encuentros Flamencos (Festival de Otoño: Autumn Festival)
October. An annual celebration of flamenco that takes place in
Teatro Isabel la Católica and Teatro del Zaidín. ❶ 958 229 344

Festival de Jazz de Granada (Granada Jazz Festival) November.
A jazz festival that attracts top names. ❷ Casa Morisca, Horno
del Oro 14 ❶ 958 215 980 Ⓦ www.jazzgranada.net

⬥ *Head to Sacromonte for lively flamenco shows*

Sport & relaxation

Granada has good sports facilities for a city of its size and it's also extremely well located for outdoor activities. In the winter you can head for the mountains to go skiing, and in summer descend on the beaches of the Costa Tropical for a variety of watersports. If you are more in the mood to relax, on the other hand, where better than an Arab bathhouse (the equivalent of Turkish baths).

Bullfighting

It is easy to condemn bullfighting as ritualised animal cruelty but it's worth taking a moment to try and understand its hold on the Spanish psyche. In the media it's treated as something between a sport and an art and attending a bullfight is respectable almost to the point of being chic. Perhaps the only thing to do is see a bullfight for yourself and make up your own mind. Granada's bullring is 1.5 km (1 mile) northwest of the city centre. The season runs from April to October.

PARTICIPATION SPORTS
Skiing

The Sierra Nevada ski resort enjoys a season that lasts until the first week of May (aided by snow cannons) with almost guaranteed sunshine and blue skies all the while. Regular skiers say it offers the best spring snow conditions in Europe. The ski-station is 32 km (20 miles) by road from Granada at an altitude of 2,100 m (6,890 ft). Its top station is at 3,300 m (10,800 ft), just 100 m (300 ft) below the summit of La Veleta, Spain's third-highest peak. Altogether there are 23 lifts serving 80 pistes totalling 84 km (52 miles). The longest run, the Pista del Águila, descends for almost 6 km (4 miles). There is also a snowboard park and a cross-country skiing circuit. On Saturday evening some of the runs are open for night-skiing. As well as hotels and restaurants the ski station has two crèches.

RELAXATION

Arab baths

Hammam Baños Arabes is a recreation of an Arab bathhouse elaborately decorated with tiled mosaics. ⓐ Calle Santa Ana 16 ⓣ 958 229 978 ⓦ www.hammamspain.com/Granada

🔺 *Pedalos at the ready on Salobreña beach, Costa Tropical*

Accommodation

Granada has a good choice of places to stay, some reasonably inexpensive. Hotels are officially ranked from one to five stars but this doesn't tell you much except the quantity of facilities; atmosphere and the standard of service do not always correspond to stars, and neither do prices. Generally cheaper are *hostales* (not to be confused with youth hostels) and *pensiones*. These are guesthouses that are likely to have en-suite rooms but not 24-hour reception or room service, and they may not offer any meals apart from breakfast. A well-cared-for, family-run *pensión* or *hostal* can be a more friendly place to stay, however, than a large modern hotel armed with all creature comforts, and they represent better value. Better hotels, *hostales* and *pensiones* have heating in winter and air conditioning in summer.

A few hotels are located on the same hill as the Alhambra, which makes them convenient for visiting the city's main monument but they are not so handy for the city centre below. The Albaicín has many charming small places to stay but many of them are on steep and narrow streets where buses, cars and taxis do not reach, and you might have to walk to get to them. City

---

PRICE RATING

The price symbols indicate the approximate price of an en suite room for two people for one night in high season, including tax:

£ = under €60;   **££** = €60–120;   **£££** = more than €120

centre hotels are mainly modern and functional; their location offers a strategic base from which it is easy to get to the rest of the city, but note that some streets may be noisy day and night.

If you want guaranteed peace and quiet, there are several hotels in Granada's rural hinterland but you'll have to be prepared to commute in for sightseeing.

HOTELS

Camino Real £ Located on the new access road to the Alhambra, this *hostal* run by an English-speaking family is also convenient for the Sierra Nevada. One of the ten rooms is equipped for the physically disabled. ⓐ Avenida Santa María de la Alhambra 2–1A ⓣ 958 210 057 ⓦ www.hostalcaminoreal.com

Fonda Sanchez £ Two minutes' walk from the Gran Vía and almost as close to the cathedral, this small hotel has simple, well-lit rooms at a very good price for such a central location. ⓐ Plaza Universidad 1–2 ⓣ 958 278 235 ⓦ www.fondasanchez.com

Casa de Federico ££ A small hotel not far from the cathedral, with views of the Alhambra and Albaicín from its terrace. ⓐ Horno de Marina 13 ⓣ 958 208 534 ⓦ www.casadefederico.com

Palacio de Santa Inés ££ A charming hotel in a restored old mansion at the bottom of the Albaicín. The patio is decorated with murals thought to be by a disciple of Raphael. Some of the rooms have views of the Alhambra. ⓐ Cuesta de Santa Inés 9 ⓣ 958 22 23 62 ⓦ www.palaciosantaines.com

⬤ *The attractive lobby at the Zaguán hotel*

Santa Isabel la Real ££ A new boutique hotel in an historic building at the top of the Albaicín. It has distant views of the Alhambra from the top of its patio. ⓐ Santa Isabel la Real 19 ⓣ 958 294 658 ⓦ www.hotelsantaisabellareal.com

Zaguán ££ Pleasant hotel in a 16th-century building in which the rooms have views of the Alhambra. It has a bar-cum-coffee-shop, but no restaurant. ⓐ Carrera del Darro 23 ⓣ 958 215 730 ⓦ www.hotelzaguan.com

Parador de Granada £££ One of the jewels in the state-run chain of Parador hotels, this one has an incomparable setting beside the Alhambra and for this reason it is both expensive and usually fully booked. Reserve well ahead to ensure a room. ⓐ Real de la Alhambra ⓣ 958 221 440 ⓦ www.parador.es

SELF-CATERING (SHORT LETS)

Cuevas El Abanico £ A suite of self-contained one- or two-bedroom caves with tiled floors and whitewashed walls, each with its own kitchen and some with terraces. Like all caves, these enjoy a constant temperature: cool in summer; warm in winter. The minimum stay is normally two days. ⓐ Verea de Enmedio 89, Sacromonte ⓣ 958 226 199 ⓦ www.el-abanico.com

El Numero 8 £ An Albaicín house divided into delightful self-contained apartments for the independent traveller. There is a shared roof terrace from which there are views of the Alhambra. ⓐ La Casa de Rafa (near Aljibe de las Tomasas – call from the square to be escorted to the house) ⓣ 958 220 682 ⓦ www.elnumero8.com

YOUTH HOSTELS

Oasis Backpackers Hostel £ A very cheap place to stay but nevertheless with good facilities if you are happy to crash in a dormitory (with en-suite bathroom). Sheets, breakfast, internet access, tea and coffee and the use of a personal safe are all included in the price. ⓐ Placeta Correo Viejo 3 (in the lower part of the Albaicín just above Calle Elvira) ⓣ 958 215 848 ⓦ www.oasisgranada.com

CAMPSITES

Camping María Eugenia The closest campsite to the city, about 3 km (2 miles) from the centre. Open year round. ⓐ Avenida de Andalucía 190 (A329 from Granada towards Málaga) ⓣ 958 200 606 ⓦ www.vayacamping.net/mariaeugenia

🔺 *Interesting murals at the Palacio de Santa Inés*

THE BEST OF GRANADA

Whether you have days of leisure to spare or a few hours to cram everything essential into, these are some of the sights and activities you'll probably want to fit into your stay.

TOP 10 ATTRACTIONS

- **Albaicín** This labyrinthine former Muslim quarter on the hill opposite the Alhambra is a place to explore on foot, taking your time (see page 88).

- **Alhambra** The incomparable palace-fortress, exquisitely decorated within, is Granada's must-see monument (see page 60).

- **The Alpujarras** An area of deep valleys with long green slopes on the other side of the Sierra Nevada from the city. Scenic walking country and cute villages (see page 117).

- **Capilla Real** The two monarchs who unified Spain lie under magnificent sepulchres in this royal chapel next to the cathedral (see page 73).

- **Corral del Carbón** A former *caravanserai* (roadside inn). Small and discreet but redolent of times gone by (see page 79).

- **Flamenco** The emblematic music and dance of southern Spain comes in many forms but is always performed with passion (see page 98).

- **Generalife** The gardens of this palace connected to the Alhambra (although they can be visited separately) are among the best in Spain (see page 69).

- **Sacromonte** Many people live in caves in Granada's traditional gypsy quarter that winds along a pretty valley (see page 94).

- **Skiing** Europe's southernmost ski resort – and Spain's highest – is close to the city. It offers excellent spring snow conditions and guaranteed sunshine (see page 35).

- **Tapas bars** The city has endless bars in all sizes and styles all serving tapas – tasty snacks – usually free with each drink you order (see page 29).

⬤ *Moorish tiles in the Palacio de Comares, Alhambra*

HALF-DAY: GRANADA IN A HURRY

With only a morning or an afternoon the only way to spend it is in the Alhambra and even then you won't see it all so concentrate on the Royal Palaces. Make sure you have reserved your ticket before arriving.

1 DAY: TIME TO SEE A LITTLE MORE

You might want to rush around the Alhambra in the morning or afternoon but you'd be better off devoting most of the day to getting there, around it and back. A stroll in the less hectic Albaicín quarter would make a good contrast and you'll certainly want to fit in a few tapas bars at midday and/or in the evening.

2–3 DAYS: SHORT CITY-BREAK

Allow the better part of one day to see the Alhambra and Generalife properly and build your visit around that. If you can,

THE SIGN OF THE POMEGRANATE

Everywhere you go in Granada you'll see the same symbol repeated over and over again, appearing everywhere from bank logos to manhole covers: a pomegranate fruit so ripe that it splits open to reveal the succulent pips within. Although the word for pomegranate in Spanish is *granada*, this is only a coincidence as the name of the city has a different derivation. The conquerors of the Moorish kingdom incorporated the pomegranate into their own coat of arms as part of the spoils of victory (and from there it found its way onto Spain's national coat of arms).

go up to the Albaicín first and admire the view of the Alhambra from it. You'll also want to spend a few hours in the city centre, visiting the Capilla Real and the Corral del Carbón and doing some shopping. Two nights will give you time to hop around several tapas bars and even find a favourite one.

LONGER: ENJOYING GRANADA TO THE FULL

With a week or more you'll have time to fit in everything you want to see and do. If this is your first visit to southern Spain, you'll probably want to get out of the city altogether and perhaps go down to the coast for one day and to Córdoba to see its famous mosque, which makes the ideal complement to the Alhambra.

● Don't miss the stunning Generalife gardens and palace

Something for nothing

To see the best of Granada you don't need to spend much money and with a little imagination you can have a great time on a shoestring budget. It is a great city just to walk around – the atmosphere and the views of the Alhambra are free. It's not difficult to devise a two- or three-day itinerary for strolling around streets and squares with frequent stops to watch street life go by from different angles. You can easily spend a day alone meandering around the delightful streets of the Albaicín and continuing to Sacromonte, buying ingredients for a sandwich to eat in some shady little square on the way. Turning pennilessness into a virtue, you can concentrate your time on seeking out the less common sights – old Arab gateways, walls, cisterns and the like – that other visitors don't bother to go and look for.

True, you won't see the inside of the Alhambra if you can't afford the price of the entrance ticket but you can still amble around the parts of the fortress, which are open to everyone, and if you are an EU citizen you can visit the Alhambra's museum in the Palacio Carlos V for free. You can also visit the Museo Arqueológico (Archaeological Museum) and the old bathhouse of El Bañuelo down below in the Darro valley for free.

Other sights that are free to get into are the Corral del Carbón, the Casa Museo Max Moreau (the house of a Belgian artist in the Albaicín), the Palacio de Dar al-Horra (also in the Albaicín), the Museo de Artes y Costumbres Populares (a folk museum) in the Casa de los Tiros and the Centro de Arte Contemporáneo José Guerrero (a gallery of contemporary art).

As a bonus, if you happen to be in Granada during a fiesta – especially Holy Week or the Corpus Christi fair – you have all the free outdoor entertainment you could ask for.

🔺 *Head up to the Alhambra for fantastic views*

When it rains

You're unlikely to get rain on a summer visit to Granada but you may well get a shower or a downpour if you are here between autumn and spring. While the city is certainly not at its best under overcast skies, and with rain drizzling down the back of your neck, there are ways to modify your itinerary in response to the weather. You won't be much interested in squares in the Albaicín or restaurant terraces with views of the Alhambra, but there are other things to do and see. If you have reserved tickets for the Alhambra you won't be able to change your plans at the last minute and unfortunately you won't see the place looking its best. Parts of the monument are, however, under cover – you'll just have to put off the Generalife gardens until another time.

The main change to your visit will be that you will have to get around by bus and hop between shelters. The city doesn't have any large museums in which to lose yourself for long periods but you could pass an hour in the Museo Arqueológico and another in the folk museum in the Casa de los Tiros. The Capilla Real and cathedral are other dry sights in the centre. Another, leisurely, way to avoid the weather is to go to an Arab bathhouse (see page 36).

In the city centre you can hop between shops across the narrow streets but a safer bet is to go to the department store of El Corte Inglés, where you can while away a few hours' browsing.

Another option is to buy a copy of *Tales of the Alhambra* (see page 64) and sit reading it in a café. If you can last until evening falls, you'll then be able to link up a series of tapas bars and bars with live music and barely notice the weather as you drift between them.

⬥ Spend a rainy hour or two at the Museo Arqueológico

On arrival

Granada is a small city, easy to get into and out of and to find your way around. It is worth allowing yourself an hour or so at the beginning of your stay to familiarise yourself with the layout of the streets, squares and sights, and the minibus routes to the Albaicín and Sacromonte and the Alhambra.

TIME DIFFERENCES
Spain follows Central European Time (CET). From late March to late September the clocks are put ahead by one hour. In the Spanish summer, at 12.00, time at home is as follows:

Australia Eastern Standard Time 20.00; Central Standard Time 19.30; Western Standard Time 18.00
New Zealand 22.00
South Africa 12.00
UK 11.00
USA and Canada Newfoundland Time 07.30; Atlantic Canada Time 07.00; Eastern Time 06.00; Central Time 05.00; Mountain Time 04.00; Pacific Time 03.00; Alaska 02.00

ARRIVING
By air
Granada's airport is Federico García Lorca (international code: GRX), 17 km (10 miles) from the city on the A92 motorway towards Antequera and Málaga. There is a bus from the airport's arrivals area to the Gran Vía de Colón in the centre of Granada. The only alternative is a taxi. ❶ 958 245 200 ⓦ www.aena.es

There is a much larger choice of flights to Málaga airport, which is 130 km (80 miles) away. There are buses from Málaga bus station to Granada approximately every hour during the day, the journey taking about two hours. ☎ 952 048 484 ⓦ www.aena.es

By rail

Granada's railway station is off Avenida de la Constitución, about 1.5 km (1 mile) west of the city centre. ⓐ Avenida Andaluces ☎ 958 271 272 (for train information ☎ 958 240 202) Ⓝ Bus: 4, 6 or 11

Services are operated by the national rail company RENFE. ☎ 902 240 202 ⓦ www.renfe.es

Granada is a stop on the route of the private luxury train, the Al Andalus Expreso. ☎ 902 169 900 ⓦ www.alandalusexpreso.com

🔺 A Credibus card is useful if you need to make several journeys

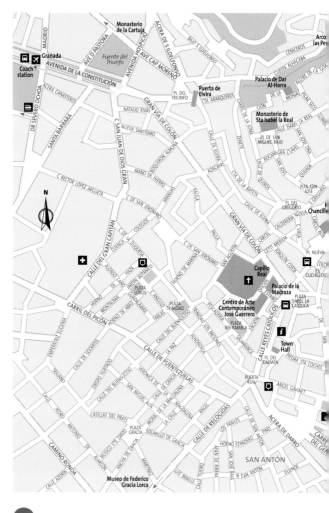

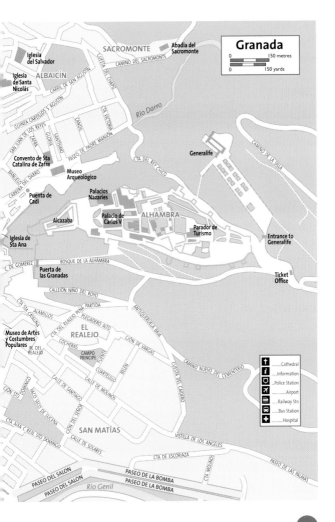

Granada

| 0 | 150 metres |
| 0 | 150 yards |

SACROMONTE
Abadía del Sacromonte

Iglesia del Salvador

Iglesia de Santa Nicolás

ALBAICÍN

CUESTA DEL CHAPIZ

CAMINO DEL SACROMONTE

CARRIL DE SAN AGUSTÍN

GUINEA CABELLOS S AGUSTÍN

SAN JUAN DE LOS REYES

ZAFRA

GLORIA

SANTISIMO

CANDIL

CTA VICTORIA

Río Darro

PASEO DE PADRE MANJON

CAMINO DE LA SILLA

Convento de Sta Catalina de Zafra

BAÑUELO DEL DARRO

Museo Arqueológico

CTA DEL REY CHICO

Generalife

CARRERA DEL DARRO

Puenta de Cadí

Palacios Nazaries

ALHAMBRA

Alcazaba

Palacio de Carlos V

Iglesia de Sta Ana

Parador de Turismo

Entrance to Generalife

C. DE GOMEREZ

BOSQUE DE LA ALHAMBRA

Puerta de las Granadas

Ticket Office

CALLEJÓN NIÑO DEL ROYO

CTA STA CATALINA

ALAMILLOS

CTA DEL REALEJO PEÑA PARTIDA

PLEGADERO ALTO

ANTIQUERUELA BAJA

Museo de Artes y Costumbres Populares

EL REALEJO

PL DEL REALEJO

COCHERAS

CIÓN DE VARGAS

CAMINO NUEVO DEL CEMENTERIO

CALLE DE SANTIAGO

CAMPO PRINCIPE

CUARTELILLO

BELEN

FUENTE

CALLE DE MOLINOS

CUESTA DEL CAIDERO

CIÓN STO DOMINGO

PACO CIÓN DE LUCENA

CTA AIXA C REAL STO DOMINGO

CIÓN DEL SEÑOR

SAN MATÍAS

CALLE DE SOLARES

VISTILLA DE LOS ANGELES

CTA DE ESCORIAZA

CTA MOLINOS

PASEO DE LAS PALMAS

PASEO DEL SALON

PASEO DEL SALON

PASEO DE LA BOMBA

PASEO DE LA BOMBA

Río Genil

✝	Cathedral
🛈	Information
👮	Police Station
✈	Airport
🚆	Railway Stn
🚌	Bus Station
✚	Hospital

53

By coach

The coach station is 2.5 km (1¹/₂ miles) northwest of the centre past the bullring. ⓐ Carretera de Jaén ⓣ 958 185 480 ⓝ Bus: 3 or 33

Driving

If you have to drive into Granada it's best to have a secure parking place lined up and head straight for it. Avoid rush hours and driving in the narrow streets of the Albaicín or the city centre. If there is a quieter time to enter or leave the city by car it is during the lunch break, around 15.00–16.00.

FINDING YOUR FEET

Granada is a lively, busy city and inevitably it has its criminals on the look-out for easy prey. That said, you should have no problems if you always keep your bag and camera close to you and don't stop in a dark alley to look at your map.

ORIENTATION

Granada's main axes are the Gran Vía de Colón and the Calle Reyes Católicos, which meet at the Plaza Isabel la Católica. To the north of here is Plaza Nueva, from where you can get to the Alhambra on foot or by minibus. To the south is another important crossroads, Puerta Real, on which stands the central post office – a useful landmark.

GETTING AROUND

The best way to get from sight to sight is to walk, but to reach the Alhambra, Sacromonte, the upper parts of the Albaicín or outlying sights, you may want to take a bus or taxi.

Bus

You probably won't need to take many buses – see the 'Líneas Turísticas' on pages 56 and 57 for useful routes. Pay the driver on boarding. If you are going to use buses a lot, buy a Credibus swipe card from the driver. This covers nine journeys (allowing you 45 minutes to change buses if necessary) and can be topped up as often as needed. For information ☎ 958 813 750

Tour buses

A good way to see a lot in a hurry is to take an open-top City Sightseeing bus ride. Buses run around two routes with commentaries in eight languages. Tours take 1 hour 15 minutes. ⓦ www.sevillacomercio.com/cityss/principal.html

GRANADA CITY PASS (BONO TURÍSTICO)

This swipe card, valid for seven days from the date of issue, allows you one free visit each to the Alhambra (you must state the time you want to visit the Nasrid Palaces – see page 67), Generalife, Cathedral, Capilla Real (Royal Chapel), Monasterio de San Jerónimo and the Parque de Ciencias (Science Museum). It also entitles you to nine bus trips and one ticket for the tour bus, City Sightseeing. The price of the card represents a saving of about 30 per cent if you visit all the sights covered. Some hotels are part of a scheme by which you get one free card per double room. Otherwise, it is available at the Alhambra, the Capilla Real and the Caja General de Ahorros bank in Plaza Isabel la Católica, or online at ⓦ caja.caja-granada.es/bono

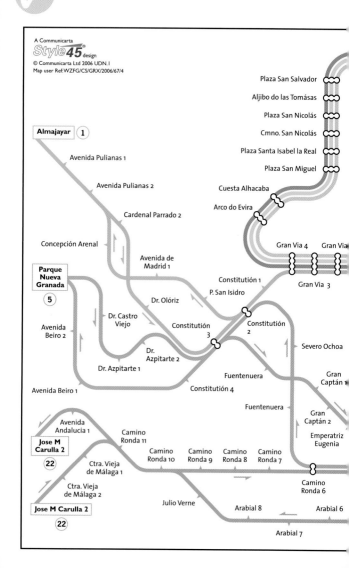

A Communicarta
Style 45 design
© Communicarta Ltd 2006 UDN. I
Map user Ref:WZFG/CS/GRX/2006/67/4

Plaza San Salvador
Aljibo do las Tomásas
Plaza San Nicolás
Cmno. San Nicolás
Plaza Santa Isabel la Real
Plaza San Miguel

Almajayar (1)

Avenida Pulianas 1

Avenida Pulianas 2

Cardenal Parrado 2

Cuesta Alhacaba

Arco do Evira

Concepción Arenal

Avenida de
Madrid 1

Gran Vía 4   Gran Vía

Parque
Nueva
Granada
(5)

Constitutión 1

Gran Vía 3

Dr. Olóriz

P. San Isidro

Dr. Castro
Viejo

Constitutión
3

Constitutión
2

Avenida
Beiro 2

Severo Ochoa

Dr.
Azpitarte 2

Gran
Captán

Dr. Azpitarte 1

Fuentenuera

Avenida Beiro 1

Constitutión 4

Fuentenuera

Gran
Captán 2

Avenida
Andalucía 1

Jose M
Carulla 2
(22)

Camino
Ronda 11

Emperatriz
Eugenia

Ctra. Vieja
de Málaga 1

Camino
Ronda 10

Camino
Ronda 9

Camino
Ronda 8

Camino
Ronda 7

Ctra. Vieja
de Málaga 2

Camino
Ronda 6

Jose M Carulla 2
(22)

Julio Verne

Arabial 8

Arabial 6

Arabial 7

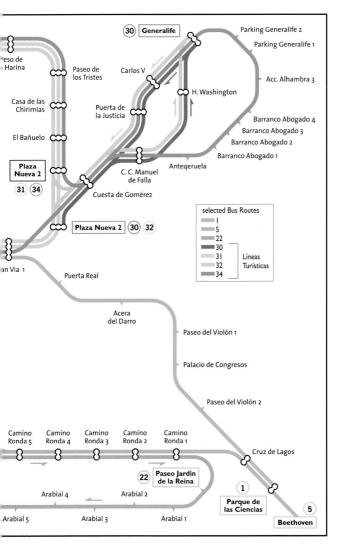

Taxis

Taxis are easily hailed on any main street and are not too costly. A green light means a taxi is for hire. The fare will be fixed by meter, which may start at a minimum charge. Tariffs increase at night and if you have luggage. For a pick-up call:

Radio Taxi ☎ 958 151 461

Taxi Genil ☎ 958 132 323

Teleradio Taxi ☎ 958 280 654

Car

Narrow streets and traffic jams mean it's not worth trying to drive around the city centre. It is best to explore on foot or by public transport or taxi. For information on car hire see page 130.

IF YOU GET LOST, TRY ...

Excuse me, do you speak English?
¿Perdone, habla usted inglés?
¿Perdoene, ahbla oosteth eengless?

Excuse me, is this the right way to the old town/the city centre/the tourist office/the station/the bus station?
¿Perdone, por aquí se va a el casco antiguo/al centro de la ciudad/oficina de turísmo/la estación de trenes/estación de autobuses?
¿Perdoneh, porr akee seh bah ah el kasko antigwo/al thentroe de la theeoodath/offeetheena deh toorismoe/la estatheeon de trenes/estatheeon dey awtoebooses?

▶ *View from San Miguel Bajo, Albaicín*

THE CITY OF
Granada

The Alhambra

No other monument anywhere has quite the allure of the world-famous fortress-palace of the Alhambra, a masterpiece of oriental art and architecture that would look more at home in the Middle East were it not planted squarely on European soil. Unsurprisingly, this wonder of the world is the most popular monument to visit in Spain and you will be wise to plan your stay in Granada around it by booking your tickets before you even arrive in the city (see visiting information on page 65).

Rather than one building, the Alhambra is an extraordinary complex of fortifications, palaces, gardens, annexes, bathhouses, prayer halls and sundry other structures dating both from the Muslim era and after. From the outside it doesn't seem to promise much but once you get inside it you will see what all the fuss is about.

The Alhambra was built by the Nasrid dynasty of kings who ruled Granada from the 13th century until the fall of the city. The most stunning part is the suite of royal palaces that mostly date from the reigns of kings Yusuf I and Muhammad V in the 14th century.

They employed the finest architects, artists and craftsmen of their day to create the most extraordinarily elaborate interior decoration, which they probably regarded as being as ephemeral as modern wallpaper.

Working without the aid of modern measuring instruments, they decorated vast surfaces with arabesques in stucco and ingenious mathematical designs of interlocking stars made from pieces of ceramic tiles in vivid colours neatly clipped to precise shapes. The idea of all this, however, was not to overwhelm the viewer but to create harmonious, endlessly repeating patterns that were easy on the eye, thus freeing the mind to think higher thoughts.

⬤ *The majestic Patio de los Arrayanes, outside the Palacio de Comares*

THE CITY

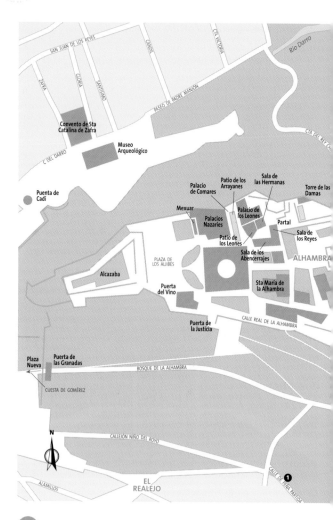

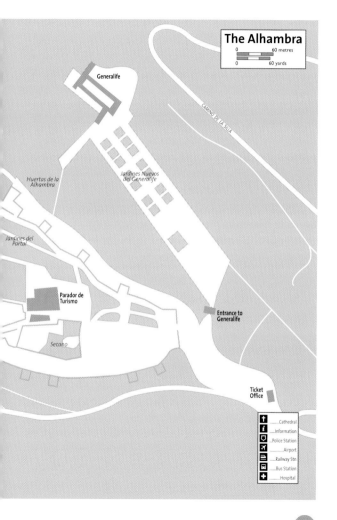

The Alhambra

0   60 metres

0   60 yards

Generalife

CAMINO DE LA SILLA

Jardines Nuevos
del Generalife

Huertas de la
Alhambra

Jardines del
Partal

Parador de
Turismo

Entrance to
Generalife

Secano

Ticket
Office

........Cathedral
........Information
........Police Station
........Airport
........Railway Stn
........Bus Station
........Hospital

Yet, ironically, what is indisputably the highest achievement of Muslim Spain was really a last creative gasp of a people at the end of their stay. While the marvels of the Alhambra were taking shape, Granada was becoming the ever more isolated, last outpost of Islam in Spain. Just over a century after the paint had dried, the civilisation that inspired such harmony and beauty came to an abrupt end.

After the Reconquest of Granada in 1492, the Alhambra suffered a fluctuating fate. Its new Christian proprietors were loath to admire the beauty of such a heathen place and they didn't know what to do with it.

Only during the 19th century did things begin to look up again for the Alhambra when it attracted the attention of travelling writers and artists who were fascinated by the oriental fantasy of it. In particular, the American writer

WASHINGTON IRVING

In 1829 the American writer Washington Irving, who is best remembered for creating the character of Rip Van Winkle, took up residence in the semi-dilapidated and much-neglected Alhambra, which was then occupied by a vestigial garrison of soldiers. Three years later he published his *Tales of the Alhambra* (widely available in the original English in Granada's souvenir shops), which makes fascinating reading before or after visiting the monument itself. It is a blend of travelogue, history and, above all, retelling of tales and myths about the Alhambra and its occupants of old.

Washington Irving lived within its walls for a while (see box) and bequeathed the world a classic book about his experiences.

In 1870 the Alhambra was finally acknowledged to be a unique, valuable and irreplaceable part of Spanish heritage. The subsequent work of restoration has sometimes been controversial and what you see today is often based on scholarly guesswork as much as actual knowledge about the work of architects and artists in 14th-century Moorish Spain.

A good way to approach the Alhambra is to look at it first from the Albaicín (see page 88), then to take a walk (or minibus) up the hill to admire its outer parts and get your bearings. Finally, ticket in hand, plunge yourself into the middle of it. For simplicity, the complex can be divided into four parts: the Alcazaba (or old citadel); the royal palaces (the highlight of the visit); the grounds of the Alhambra, including a street of shops and hotels; and the summer palace of the Generalife, which is visited chiefly for its gardens.

ⓘ Note that restoration, maintenance and repair work is being carried out continually and some parts of the monument may be temporarily closed during your visit.

How to visit

A visit to the Alhambra is best planned well in advance. You can turn up on the day and queue for a ticket at the ticket office next to the car park but you may not be able to see the best bits of the monument – the royal palaces – as visitor numbers are strictly limited. Far better is to buy your ticket by phone, online or over a bank counter (see page 66) before you arrive in Granada.

When you buy your ticket you will be allocated a half-hour time slot in which to enter the royal palaces and you should plan your visit around this. You can see other parts of the monument while you are waiting.

The best way to get to the Alhambra is on foot from Plaza Nueva, but it is a long, steep walk up the Cuesta de Gomérez and through the 16th-century Puerta de las Granadas (which is named after the pomegranates that adorn it). A minibus travels the same route from Plaza Nueva. By car, you have to approach the Alhambra along an access road from the southeast, which avoids the city centre. The ticket office is next to the car park. ❶ 902 441 221 Ⓦ www.alhambra-patronato.es or www.alhambra.org ◷ 08.30–20.00 (closes 18.00 in winter). Night visits 22.00–23.30 Tues–Sat, summer; 20.00–21.30 Tues–Sat, winter. Admission charge. Advance reservations can be made at any branch of BBVA bank or ❶ 902 224 460 or +34 915 379 178 from abroad or via the website Ⓦ www.alhambratickets.com. You can buy a maximum of five tickets at one time. You will be given a booking reference number to present at the ticket office on the day of your visit. The ticket office opens at 08.00. ⊛ Minibus: 30 or 32 from Plaza Nueva

SIGHTS & ATTRACTIONS

Puerta de la Justicia (Gate of Justice)

From the ticket office, visitors are guided along a broad path inside the Alhambra's walls but a more interesting route is to go down the road, following the outside of the walls. Ignore the first road to the right and you will come to a bend over which looms the monumental portal of the Gate of Justice, a traditional entrance to the fortress with a staggered path through it to deter invaders. There are two carvings on the outer wall of the gate: a hand (on the taller, outer horseshoe arch) and, lower down, a key with a tassel attached to it. These symbols have never been explained.

Alcazaba

The ramp from the Puerta de la Justicia brings you into the Plaza de los Aljibes (Square of the Cisterns), one side of which is formed by the Alcazaba, the oldest part of the Alhambra, which probably stands on Roman foundations. An austere fortress of walls and six towers, the Alcazaba tapers towards the apex of the hill where the Torre de la Vela (watchtower) stands guard over the city below. It offers tremendous views from its battlements over Granada's rooftops, across the ravine to the Albaicín and south to the Sierra Nevada.

Palacios Nazaríes (Nasrid Palaces)

The finest part of the Alhambra is the complex of royal (or Nasrid) palaces. There may have been as many as seven palaces in the Alhambra's heyday, but now there are essentially three interlocking suites of magnificently decorated chambers and delightful patios.

The first part of the palaces is the Mexuar, which has one open and one enclosed courtyard. This part of the Alhambra was much altered by Granada's Christian conquerors and so is not in its original state. Its main two rooms are the Hall of the Mexuar, probably used as a council chamber but later converted into a chapel, and the Golden Chamber, which, despite its suggestive name, may have been a mere waiting room for those about to have an audience with the king.

From the Mexuar you step into the long rectangular patio of the Palacio de Comares, which is known as the Patio de los Arrayanes (Courtyard of the Myrtles) because of the hedges planted beside its central pool.

At the northern end of this pond is the chamber which makes the greatest impression on visitors, the Salón de Embajadores (Hall of the Ambassadors), also called the Throne Room. Its ceiling is made of more than 8,000 separate pieces of coloured wood.

A humble doorway leads from the Comares patio to the exquisite Patio de los Leones (Courtyard of the Lions), a cloister of slender columns and beautiful filigree decorations. The name comes from the fountain in the middle, in which a bowl is supported on 12 rather crudely carved beasts. Off the courtyard are the splendidly ornate Sala de los Reyes (Hall of the Kings), Sala de las Dos Hermanas (Hall of the Two Sisters) and Sala de los Abencerrajes (Hall of the Abencerrajes). This last has a star-shaped cupola dripping with *mocarabes* – stalactite stucco mouldings that are supposed to recall the cave in which Muhammad received his inspiration for the Koran. There are supposedly irremovable stains of blood in the floor/fountain of the Hall of the Abencerrajes, as evidence of the murder of members of one clan by another, but these are merely reddish veins in the marble.

You leave the rooms occupied by Washington Irving and pass through two courtyards that were added to the Alhambra in the

16th century. Off the second courtyard is the palace bathhouse, which is lit by star-shaped holes in the ceiling and has some surviving tilework on the walls.

Partal and the Medina

The area behind the Palacio de los Leones is called the Partal and its most notable feature is the Torre de las Damas (Tower of the Ladies), which is little more than a portico standing beside a large pond. Paths lead from here past several towers along the Alhambra's northern walls towards the entrance to the Generalife. The best way to return from the Generalife is via the broad path from the ticket office, which passes the ruins of the medina, once a city of courtiers' palaces and the houses of soldiers and servants.

Generalife

The Alhambra may look like the sort of luxurious residence a sultan would never want to leave, but he also had a second home further up the hill, the Generalife, which was far enough away from his daily work of running the kingdom for him to be able to relax, but still close enough to be able to attend to any urgent affairs of state. In front of the palace is a very long, much photographed pond with twin rows of fountains feeding it. Around the palace are extensive formal gardens although most of what you see is the result of rebuilding and reshaping according to modern tastes. The most unusual feature is the Escalera del Agua (Water Staircase), in which a stream is ingeniously divided and fed, gurgling down the two handrails.

CULTURE

Palacio de Carlos V

In 1626 Spain's King Carlos I (better known as Holy Roman Emperor Charles V) ordered the construction of a palace within the walls of the Alhambra, which involved the demolition of some existing buildings. Anywhere else and it would have to be considered as one of the greatest works of the Spanish Renaissance, but it is undeniably out of character here and put into the aesthetic shade by the Moorish palaces next door. The palace is visited separately from the Alhambra. It contains two museums: the **Museo de la Alhambra**, which displays works of Islamic art, and the **Museo de Bellas Artes** (Museum of Fine Art). Next to the palace is a church and next to this is a small but pleasing bathhouse.

○ *Visit the museums of the Palacio de Carlos V*

Museo de la Alhambra ☎ 958 227 527 🕐 09.00–14.00 Tues–Sat.
Admission charge but free for EU citizens
Museo de Bellas Artes ☎ 958 221 449
ⓦ www.museosdeandalucia.es 🕐 09.00–14.00 Mon–Fri.
Admission charge but free for EU citizens

RETAIL THERAPY

Cuesta de Gomérez The steep street heading up to the
Alhambra from Plaza Nueva is lined with mostly indifferent
souvenir shops specialising in ceramics and marquetry. It is a
traditional location for guitar workshops but only two are left
(there are others elsewhere in Granada): J Lopez (no. 36) and
Manuel Diaz (no. 29). One of the better craft/souvenir shops is
El Suspiro (which has Granada pottery and other items).
ⓐ Cuesta de Gomérez 45 ☎ 958 229 996 🕐 11.00–20.30

Laguna Taracea If you want to buy a serious piece of craftwork,
step into this marquetry shop that has been running since 1877.
Some of the items are still made on the premises. ⓐ Calle Real
de la Alhambra 30 ☎ 958 229 019 ⓦ www.laguna-taracea.com
🕐 09.30–18.30

Librería de la Alhambra The Alhambra has three official
shops: in the ticket hall, in the Palacio de Carlos V and this
one, which is small and specialises in books about the Alhambra
and Granada, some of them in English. ⓐ Calle Real de la
Alhambra, on the corner opposite the Palacio Carlos V
🕐 09.30–19.30

Ruiz Linares This large souvenir shop is often heaving with coach parties. ⓐ Calle Real de la Alhambra 64 ⓣ 958 221 971 ⓛ 09.30–17.30

TAKING A BREAK

There aren't many places to eat within easy reach of the Alhambra. Your best bet is to either take a picnic with you (but don't eat it inside the Alhambra's grounds) or get back down to the Plaza Nueva, where there are endless bars and restaurants.

Alhambra Palace £££ ❶ A hotel across the hill from the Alhambra, with kitsch Moorish decoration. There are great views over the city from the bar's terrace, which is open to non-residents. ⓐ Peña Partida 2 ⓣ 958 221 468 ⓦ www.h-alhambrapalace.es

⬥ Pottery, paintings and plenty more at El Suspiro

The city centre

A long broad street, the Gran Vía de Colón, separates the Albaicín (see page 88) from the city centre. It meets the other principal street through the city, Calle Reyes Católicos, at Plaza Isabel la Católica. The angle formed between these is packed with the small squares and narrow streets swarming around the cathedral. Two larger squares, Plaza Bib-Rambla and Plaza Trinidad, provide some relief from the dense mass of bars, shops and apartment blocks.

Across the other side of Reyes Católicos the streets behind the Plaza del Carmen (on which stands the town hall) lead towards the district of El Realejo. There are few sights to tempt you in this direction in the daytime but plenty of bars that might attract you at night.

From Puerta Real, at the end of Reyes Católicos, the city centre continues down the busy streets of Recogidas (towards the inner ring road, the Camino de Ronda) and the Acera del Darro (towards the banks of the Río Genil). Again, it won't be sightseeing that leads you down here, but bars and shops.

SIGHTS & ATTRACTIONS

Capilla Real (Royal Chapel)

The conquerors of Muslim Granada and unifiers of Spain, King Fernando and Queen Isabel, better known as the Reyes Católicos (Catholic Monarchs), are buried in this Gothic chapel especially built for the purpose. Although much smaller than the cathedral next door, it is far more interesting to visit. Steps take you down from the entrance hall (Lonja) into the chapel proper,

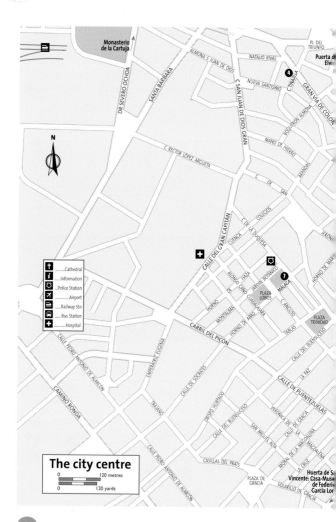

Monasterio de la Cartuja

PL. DEL TRIUNFO

NATALIÓ RIVAS

Puerta d Elvi

ALMONA S. JUAN DE DIOS

DR SEVERO OCHOA

SANTA BÁRBARA

C SAN JUAN DE DIOS GRAN

NUEVA SANTÍSIMO

CTNALLA

GRAN VÍA DE COLÓN

BOQUERÓN ALMONA

ARANDAS

MANO DE HIERRO

C. RECTOR LÓPEZ ARGUETA

N

C DE SAN

COLEGIOS

JERONI

C DE LA DUQUESA

C ANGUTO

CUENCA

CALLE DEL GRAN CAPITÁN

PLAZA

ALONSO CANO DE

JARDÍN BOTÁNICO

MÁLAGA

7

HORNO DE MAR

PLAZA LOBOS

GUADALAHARA

MONTALBÁN

HORNO DE ABAD

TABLAS

PLAZA TRINIDAD

HORNO

CARRIL DEL PICÓN

CALLE DE BUENSUCESO

EMPERATRIZ EUGENIA

LA PAZ

CALLE PEDRO ANTONIO DE ALARCÓN

CALLE DE SOROATES

OBISPO HURTADO

CALLE DEL BUENSUCESO

VERÓNICA DE GRACIA

CALLE DE PUENTEZUELAS

TRAJANO

SAN MIGUEL ALTA

CALLE DE

CAMINO RONDA

MORAL DE LA MAGDALENA

CALLE PEDRO ANTONIO DE ALARCÓN

CASILLAS DEL PRATS

PLAZA DE GRACIA

LA CRUZ

Huerta de S Vincente: Casa-Muse de Federi García Lor

SOLARILLO DE GRACIA

Legend:
- ✝ ....Cathedral
- i ....Information
- 🛡 ....Police Station
- ✈ ....Airport
- 🚆 ....Railway Stn
- 🚌 ....Bus Station
- ✚ ....Hospital

The city centre

0 ————— 120 metres

0 ————— 120 yards

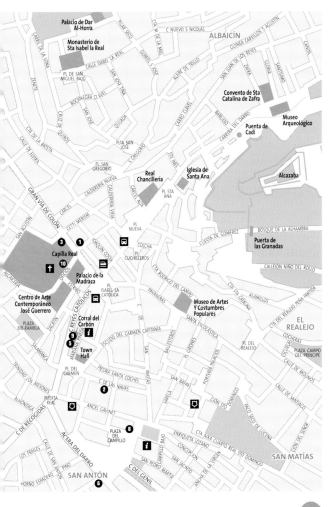

which has three impressively ornate iron grilles. Beyond the largest of these are two sepulchres, one for the Catholic Monarchs and one for their daughter, the unfortunately named Juana la Loca (Joanna the Mad), and her husband Felipe el Hermoso (Philip the Fair). A large altarpiece looks down on the sepulchres. Below ground is a crypt where the lead coffins of all four royals – together with that of a prince who died in infancy – lie together. You leave the chapel through the sacristy, where works of primitive Flemish art are on display along with Fernando's sword and Isabel's crown.

🅐 Oficios 12 ☎ 958 229 239 🕐 10.30–13.00, 16.00–19.00 Mon–Sat, 11.00–13.00, 16.00–19.00 Sun 🆆 www.capillarealgranada.com. Admission charge

JUANA LA LOCA

History hasn't been kind to Fernando and Isabel's daughter who is buried with them in the Capilla Real. She will forever be remembered by the unkind epithet of Juana la Loca (Joanna the Mad), although it is far from certain that she was actually insane. Lovesick and grief-stricken, certainly, which is a better explanation for her reckless behaviour. When her adored but serially unfaithful husband Felipe (Philip the Fair) died young, she set off with his body on a journey from Burgos in northern Spain to Granada, travelling by night and opening the coffin every now and then to gaze at his decomposing remains. She and her grisly cargo didn't reach Granada according to schedule, but they both ended up being buried here much later.

Casa de los Tiros: Museo de Artes y Costumbres Populares (House of Shots folk museum)

You might want to just admire this 16th-century mansion from the outside, as the façade is a delightful bit of restrained Gothic, with the figures of five Greek heroes embedded in it. It's said to get its popular name – 'the House of Shots' – from the cannons that protrude from the battlements at the top of the façade, but a legend (wholly without foundation) has a more colourful explanation. In 1723 the Marquis of El Salar ran a young student through with his sword in a duel after the latter had offended the lady with whom he was in love. Rather than face the dishonour of trial and execution, the marquis shut himself up in this house and shot himself twice. The next day a letter arrived saying that he was to be pardoned for his crime but it was, of course, too late. Exactly 100 years later an inhabitant of the house is said to have knocked down a hollow-sounding wall and stumbled into the very room where the marquis had taken his own life; it had been sealed up exactly as it had been on that fateful day.

However it got its nickname, the building is now officially a museum dealing with the history of Granada. Among the exhibits there's a fascinating map dated 1796, which is effectively an A–Z guide to the pre-industrial city. Room 4, meanwhile, deals with 19th-century Romantic travellers, including Washington Irving (see page 64).

ⓐ Pavaneras 19 ☎ 958 221 072 🕒 11.00–14.00, 17.00–21.00 Tues–Sat, 11.00–14.00 Sun

Catedral de Granada (Granada Cathedral)

Granada's central church was begun on the site of the city's main mosque shortly after the Reconquest. It is considered a prime example of Spanish Renaissance architecture but is more impressive outside than it is inside and if you are pressed for time, or don't care for too many churches, see the Capilla Real next door instead.

It officially stands on the Gran Vía, but you could walk past it unless you were looking for the wrought-iron gateway leading to it. Curiously, its main façade looks the other way, onto an inconspicuous pedestrianised square off the corner of the more expansive Plaza Bib-Rambla.

◆ *The magnificent Catedral and Capilla Real*

The most impressive thing about the interior is its immense volume, which is divided into a nave and four aisles by stout white columns. Various artistic treasures are distributed around the building including 16th-century Flemish stained-glass windows depicting the Passion, two life-sized coloured statues of Fernando and Isabel (the Catholic Monarchs) kneeling in pious prayer, golden statues of the apostles, a statue of St James on horseback, a superb late Gothic doorway and many large paintings by Juan de Sevilla, Alonso Cano and others.

ⓐ Gran Vía de Colón (entrance on Calle Oficios) ❶ 958 222 959 ⏰ 10.45–13.30, 16.00–19.00 Mon–Sat, Sun afternoon only. Admission charge

ⓘ Around the cathedral and Capilla Real you may be approached by one of several gypsy women who make a living out of thrusting sprigs of rosemary into the hands of unwary visitors, telling them it is a gift. If you accept the rosemary, the woman will insist on telling your fortune and demand payment. If you are not in the mood, politely decline the rosemary and keep walking.

Corral del Carbón (Coal House)

This 14th-century Arab *caravanserai* is the only such building surviving in Spain. It was originally an inn and warehouse for travelling merchants but was turned into a charcoal burners' depot – hence the name – and, in the 16th century, into a theatre. In some ways it is this last use that suits it best and it is still used as a venue for a programme of summer concerts. From the street an impressive horseshoe-arched gateway lets you

through into a courtyard of three storeys of galleries looking
down on a small fountain. It's a very peaceful corner of the city –
only a step away from the busy Calle Reyes Católicos – if you are
lucky enough to get it to yourself for a few minutes.

ⓐ Mariana Pineda ⓣ no phone ⓛ 10.30–13.30, 17.00–20.00
Mon–Fri, 10.30–14.00 Sat

Huerta de San Vicente: Casa-Museo de Federico García Lorca (San Vicente Gardens: house and museum of Federico García Lorca)

The house where the poet and playwright Federico García Lorca
(see box, page 22) spent his summers and wrote some of his
best-loved pieces, including the play *Blood Wedding*, used to be
2 km (1 mile) outside the city but now stands in its own park
between Calle Arabial and the ring road. Visitors are taken on
a 30-minute guided tour, which explains Lorca's life and work.

ⓐ Calle Virgen Blanca ⓣ 958 258 466
ⓦ www.huertadesanvicente.com ⓛ 10.00–14.30 Tues–Sun, July &
Aug; 10.00–12.30, 18.00–19.30 Tues–Sun, Apr, May, June & Sept;
10.00–12.30, 16.00–18.30 Tues–Sun, Oct–Mar. Admission charge

Monasterio de la Cartuja

It's only worth making the trek out to this 16th- to 17th-century
monastery if you have a taste for the excesses of baroque
decoration. If you have, you will love the florid white stucco in
the church and sacristy, which are considered among the finest
examples of Churrigueresque – an extreme version of baroque.

ⓐ Paseo de Cartuja ⓣ 958 161 932 ⓛ 10.00–13.30, 14.00–19.30
(15.00–18.30 in winter) ⓝ Bus: line 8. Admission charge

Plaza Bib-Rambla

This large rectangular square occupies the site of an old Arab gateway long since demolished. Shaded by lime trees, it is a

⏶ *Find a shady spot to cool down in the Plaza Bib-Rambla*

pleasant space to take a break from shopping in the
neighbouring streets. There are bars and cafés around it with
tables set out on the pavements, some of them serving
chocolate con churros (hot chocolate and batter sticks to dunk),
which is eaten for breakfast, as a snack in the evening, or, during
fiestas, at just about any time of the day or night. In the middle
of the square is a fountain taken from a demolished convent,
which rests on the shoulders of four grotesque giants.

Plaza Isabel la Católica

This square is the closest thing Granada has to a central focal
point but it's not an inviting place to hang around. It is named
after the queen of Castile who, along with her husband
Fernando, captured Granada from the Moors in 1492. The statue
in the middle of the square is a 19th-century work by Mariano
Benillure, and it shows Isabel with that other protagonist of the
year 1492, Christopher Columbus (Cristobal Colón in Spanish).

El Realejo

This area is sometimes described as the former Jewish quarter
of the city but there is no evidence for it having been. In 1497
the city council ordered a swathe of streets and houses to be
flattened to form the Plaza Campo del Principe (around which it
is grouped) in honour of the marriage of the heir apparent in
that year. Sadly, he died six months after the marriage. The
square is now a centre for bars and clubs. The only other reason
to stray this way is if you want to go up to or come down from
the Alhambra on foot following a quieter route than the Cuesta
de Gomérez from Plaza Nueva. On the way you might want to

stop and look at the former residence of the Granada-born painter José Maria Rodríguez Acosta (1878–1941). The house is in a straight white modern style set off by cypress trees, but the artist accessorised it with an eclectic selection of historical artefacts (some genuine, others imitation).

Fundación Rodríguez-Acosta ❸ Callejón Niño del Rollo 8
❶ 958 227 497 ⓦ www.fundacionrodriguezacosta.com
🕔 10.00–14.00 Wed–Sun. Admission charge

CULTURE

Centro de Arte Contemporáneo José Guerrero (José Guerrero Centre of Contemporary Art)

This contemporary art gallery always has one room dedicated to the paintings of the Granada-born abstract artist (1914–91) after which it is named, but the other two main rooms and smaller

CHRISTOPHER COLUMBUS

Columbus 'sailed the ocean blue in fourteen hundred and ninety-two' but he wouldn't have done so had events the year before gone another way. It was during the protracted siege of Granada that the Genoese adventurer relentlessly importuned the queen for funds to make his voyage. He'd all but given up hope when she finally agreed to commission him. One story has it that she pawned her jewels to subsidise his three-piece fleet, but it is fairly certain she didn't do so until she was sure that the rich prize of Granada was about to fall into her hands.

spaces are dedicated to changing exhibitions of avant-garde installations, including multimedia shows.

ⓐ Oficios 8 ⓣ 958 225 185 ⓦ www.centroguerrero.org
ⓛ 11.00–14.00, 17.00–21.00 Tues–Sat, Sun mornings only

Palacio de la Madraza

Although this building across the street from the cathedral and the Capilla Real has an 18th-century façade, it is actually much older. It was originally built in the 14th century as a school for Koranic studies and, although it has been much altered since the Reconquest, it still has its original hall and *mihrab* (prayer niche). It is mainly used for artistic and cultural events.

ⓐ Oficios 14 ⓛ closed for restoration

RETAIL THERAPY

La Alacena A delicatessen that sells all good things to eat and drink made in Andalucía. ⓐ San Jerónimo 3 ⓣ 958 206 890
ⓦ www.alacena.net ⓛ 11.00–14.00, 17.00–20.00

Alcaicería This 19th-century recreation of the city's Arab silk bazaar with alleys and horseshoe arches conjuring a faux oriental feel is an inviting place to shop, but don't expect to find too many authentic granadino crafts for sale as most of the items are souvenirs for tourists. One of the better shops inside it is Artesanía Alcaicería (ⓐ stalls 1, 3 and 10 ⓣ 958 229 045
ⓦ www.alcaiceria.com), which specialises in miniature figures for Christmas cribs.

Metro International Bookshop The best stock of English books in Granada. 🄰 Calle de Gracia 31 (between Puentezuelas and Plaza de Gracia) 🄣 958 261 565 🄛 10.00–14.00, 17.00–20.30 Mon–Fri, 11.00–14.00 Sat

TAKING A BREAK

Cafés
Internacional £ ❶ There's only one thing special about this bright stripped-down cafeteria on the Gran Vía: it opens at 07.00 and so is a good place for early breakfast of orange juice, toast and coffee. 🄣 no phone 🄰 Gran Vía de Colón 12

🔺 Lose yourself in the alleyways of the Alcaiceria

Navas £ ❷ If you can't face talking to anyone or choosing from a menu, this self-service hotel cafeteria offers an inexpensive, and usually quiet, place to eat whatever you feel like eating, without any fuss. ⓐ Calle de las Navas 22–24 ❶ 958 225 959 ⓦ hotelesporcel.com

Vía Colón £ ❸ The baroque mouldings and marble counter tops may be imitation old but this is still a lovely place for a sandwich or lunch. Not a relaxing place to linger too long but it does have a terrace outside in summer. ⓐ Gran Vía de Colón 13 ❶ 958 220 752

Bars & tapas

Bodega Espadafor £ ❹ An old-fashioned bar that's well known for its tapas. ⓐ Calle Tinajilla ❶ 958 202 1389

Café Fútbol £ ❺ This bar-restaurant with terrace is famous for its ice creams and its *chocolates con churros*. ⓐ Mariana Pineda 6 ❶ 958 226 662

Taberna Casa Enrique ££ ❻ A classic near Puerta Real serving good tapas and a choice of wines. ⓐ Acera del Darro 8 ❶ 958 255 008

AFTER DARK

Restaurants

Botánico £ ❼ A cool, modern restaurant where the menu combines influences from Mexico, North Africa and Asia. ⓐ Málaga 3 ❶ 958 271 598

Chikito ££ ❽ Creative Andalucían cooking in this traditional restaurant and bar set in a lovely square. ⓐ Plaza del Campillo 9 ⓘ 958 223 364 ⓛ closed Wed

Corral del Carbón ££ ❾ This restaurant specialises in grilled meats – mainly lamb and sausages. Look for the signed photo of Federico García Lorca at one end of the bar. ⓐ Mariana Pineda 8 ⓘ 958 223 810

Sevilla £££ ❿ One of Federico García Lorca's favourite restaurants, opposite the Capilla Real. ⓐ Oficios 12 ⓘ 958 221 223

Flamenco shows
Café au Lait Puts on nightly flamenco shows ⓐ Plaza Romanilla 10 (behind the cathedral) ⓘ 958 202 047

Clubs
Granada 10 A cinema in the evening; a discotheque at night (from 00.30 to 06.00 on weekdays and 07.00 at weekends) playing disco, hip-hop, funk, Latin, salsa – you name it. ⓐ Carcel Baja 10 ⓘ 958 224 001

The Albaicín & Sacromonte

Two hills face each other across the narrow valley of the River Darro. On one stands the Alhambra; the other is occupied by the Albaicín (sometimes spelt Albayzin), the most perfectly preserved Moorish quarter in Spain. Because of the terrain it is built on, the Albaicín is characterised by narrow streets, which are usually steep and often stepped – many are called *cuesta* (meaning slope).

Most of the charm here is in wandering around and seeing what you stumble on by chance. You won't be able to miss the churches, as their bell-towers (barely disguised minarets) stand proud of all other buildings. Also conspicuous (but secretive at the same time) are the *carmines* – the typical well-to-do houses of the Albaicín, which are villas with gardens protected by high walls. Most of them you can only glimpse through their gates but some have been put to public use as restaurants and the like. Other features to look out for are the innumerable water cisterns, *aljibes*, which are organised according to an ingenious 500-year-old water-supply system.

The Albaicín is worth a leisurely visit in its own right but it also offers the best views of the Alhambra, particularly from the Plaza (or Mirador) San Nicolás outside the church of the same name. At a push you can get from the city centre to this viewpoint and back in an hour, but it would be a shame to rush it and it is certainly a good idea to allow yourself time in case you get lost (very likely) and need to find your bearings again.

There are many ways into the Albaicín but the most popular is to take Calderería Nueva from Calle Elvira (not far from the corner of Plaza Nueva), which brings you to Plaza San Gregorio. If you keep climbing in the same direction and bear uphill to your left you will eventually strike the Plaza de San Nicolás.

A more interesting route is to turn left almost immediately after leaving Plaza San Gregorio up the short street of Grifos de San José. Veer left at the end and you will be in Placeta de San José, which is overlooked by a delightful 10th-century minaret. Go uphill underneath the minaret and you'll reach the pretty Plaza de San Miguel Bajo. From here it is a straight run along Calle Isabel La Real, past the 16th- to 17th-century convent of the same name (for visits, call ☎ 958 200 688), to San Nicolás.

From Plaza San Nicolás all roads lead down to the Darro valley. If you get lost, face the Alhambra, which is visible from almost everywhere, and head downhill. This way you will strike one of Granada's most historic streets, the Carrera del Darro. Turn right and you will come to Plaza Nueva.

Beyond the Albaicín is Sacromonte, the old gypsy quarter of the city where many people still live, by choice, in caves carved out of the soft rock. There is an excellent visitor centre explaining cave life and the traditions (including flamenco music and dance) of Sacromonte.

SIGHTS & ATTRACTIONS

El Bañuelo

There's not much to see from outside unfortunately, but this Arab bath has a fine vaulted interior lit by star-shaped apertures in the ceiling. These baths were built in the 11th century and are therefore older than most of the Alhambra. The main chamber

THE CITY

🕇	.........Cathedral
i	.........Information
🚓	.........Police Station
✈	.........Airport
🚆	.........Railway Stn
🚌	.........Bus Station
✚	.........Hospital

PLTA ALMONA

PL LARGA

Arco de las Pesas

VEREDILLA DE SAN CRISTOBAL

CENICEROS

BAJO S ILDEFONSO

CUESTA ALHACABA

AGIRE DE LA GITANA

CJON CAMPANAS

PLTA DE LAS MINAS

CTA MAPA DE LA MIEL

PL SAN NICOLAS

PL DEL TRIUNFO

Puerta de Elvira

CTA ABARQUEROS

Palacio de Dar Al-Horra

DE LAS MONJAS

PILAR SECO

C NUEVO DE SAN

5

CARRIL DE LA LONA

CJON

Monasterio de Sta Isabel la Real

CALLE ISABEL LA REAL

GUMIEL S JOSE

ALJIBE DE TRUJILLO

C

CALLE ELVIRA

ZENETE

4

PL DE SAN MIGUEL BAJO

SAN JOSE FINA

CJON ALJIB

GRAN VIA DE COLON

AZACAYAS

CROON NEGRA CLAVEL

SAN JOSE

QUIJADA

CARBO CERR

ARANDAS

CTA DE LA BATTIA

CRUZ DE QUIROS

PLTA DE SAN JOSE

PAULA

S GREGORIO

STA INES

CALLE ELVIRA

PL SAN GREGORIO

Iglesia de Santa Ana

PENDILLAS STA PAULA MARQUES

CALDERERIA NUEVA

CARCEL ALT

PL STA ANA

PAULA

1

CALDERERIA VIEJA

Real Chancilleria

6

GRAN VIA DE COLON

CARCEL

CETTI MERIEM

HOSPITAL D

HORNO HAZA/NA

C DE SAN JERONIMO

JOAQUIN COSTA

PLAZA NUEVA

SAN AGUSTIN

2

PLAZA NUEVA

COLCHA

Capilla Real

🕇

🚌

🚆

PL CUCHILLEROS

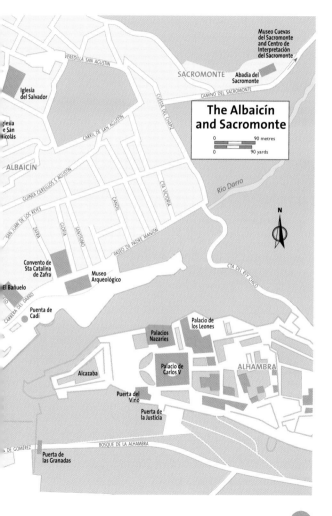

VEREDILLA SAN AGUSTÍN

Museo Cuevas
del Sacromonte
and Centro de
Interpretación
del Sacromonte

SACROMONTE   Abadía del
Sacromonte

Iglesia
del Salvador

CAMINO DEL SACROMONTE

glesia
e San
Nicolás

CARRIL DE SAN AGUSTÍN

CUESTA DEL CHAPIZ

The Albaicín
and Sacromonte

0 _____ 90 metres
0 _____ 90 yards

ALBAICÍN

GUINEA CARRILLOS S AGUSTÍN

CTA. VICTORIA

CANDIL

Río Darro

SAN JUAN DE LOS REYES

GLORIA

ZAFRA

SANTÍSIMO

N

PASEO DE PADRE MANJÓN

CTA. DEL REY CHICO

Convento de
Sta Catalina
de Zafra

Museo
Arqueológico

El Bañuelo

CARRERA DEL DARRO

Palacio de
los Leones

Puerta de
Cadí

Palacios
Nazaríes

ALHAMBRA

Alcazaba

Palacio de
Carlos V

Puerta del
Vino

Puerta de
la Justicia

A DE GÓMEREZ

BOSQUE DE LA ALHAMBRA

Puerta de
las Granadas

has incongruous columns supporting carved capitals that were brought from elsewhere, possibly from Córdoba.

ⓐ Carrera del Darro ⓣ 958 027 800 ⓛ 10.00–14.00 Tues–Sat

Calle Elvira & Puerta de Elvira

The narrow, winding Calle Elvira shadows the Gran Vía de Colón from Plaza Nueva to Plaza del Triunfo: the one a distinctly indirect oriental route; the other a no-nonsense, broad, modern

◓ *The star-shaped vents inside El Bañuelo*

avenue. Guarding the Plaza del Triunfo end of the street is the
Puerta de Elvira, which was the main entrance through the
walls of the Albaicín. Sadly, bits of it were progressively removed
after the Reconquest until only the outer part was left.

Carrera del Darro

The Carrera del Darro runs along the valley of the River Darro,
which separates the Alhambra from the Albaicín. There are
various historic buildings along the way, including El Bañuelo,
the Museo Arqueológico and two convents. Hovering over the
river is an impressive 11th-century half-arch, the Puente de Cadí
or Puerta de los Tableros, which is thought to have been part
of both a dam and a military route between the Alhambra
and Albaicín.

Plaza Larga

The focal point of the upper Albaicín is this square, which is
home to a daily market. A small dog-legged gateway, the Arco
de las Pesas (Arch of the Weights), connects it with the
unnoticeable Placeta de las Minas. The name is thought to have
been bestowed on it because the fraudulent weights of
unscrupulous traders were hung here as an example to others.

Plaza Nueva

Unlike most other Spanish cities, Granada hasn't got a single
main square or *plaza mayor* around which the layout of the city
revolves. This elongated space between the Alhambra and the
Albaicín, however, shares the function with the adjacent Plaza
Isabel la Católica. It is really three squares in one, with Plaza

Santa Ana seamlessly joined to its top end (looked down on by a Moorish-style church of the same name) and Plaza Cuchilleros stuck onto it at the bottom. Three important roads meet here: the narrow and winding old road of Calle Elvira, the Carrera del Darro and the Cuesta de Gomérez, which ascends towards the Alhambra. The city's main tourist office is off the corner of the square near the church. The most conspicuous building on Plaza Nueva is the 16th-century Real Chancillería (Royal Chancery) or law courts.

Plaza San Nicolás

The Plaza San Nicolás offers the classic view of the Alhambra with the (usually) snow-capped Sierra Nevada as a background. The church it is named after stands in the middle of the square on the site of one of the Albaicín's main mosques. As if by a touch of historical irony, beside it now stands the Mezquita Mayor, a mosque serving Granada's latter-day Muslim community.

Mezquita Mayor 🕐 10.00–14.00, 18.00–21.00 summer; 10.00–14.00, 15.00–19.00 winter, but times may change during Muslim festivals

SACROMONTE

Granada's 'Holy Mount' received its name after the Reconquest, largely because of several lead 'books' supposedly found in a cave at the end of the 16th century. Written in Arabic, they related the martyrdom of the apocryphal St Cecil (San Cecilio), first bishop of Granada, who lived during Roman times, but they were eventually judged to be fakes. However, an abbey (*abadía*) was built in the 17th century, which became a focal point of the

Counter-Reformation in Andalucía. Beneath it are the catacombs where St Cecil is said to have been martyred.

Today, Sacromonte is better known as Granada's cave and gypsy quarter and the place to go to see and hear flamenco. Whatever draws you this way, you will certainly find a quarter of the city very different from all others and the best place to learn about its life and traditions is the **Museo Cuevas del Sacromonte** or **Centro de Interpretación del Sacromonte**, a complex of ten caves with displays on how people have traditionally lived and worked in Sacromonte as well as on its

THE RETURN OF ISLAM

After the Reconquest of Spain, the new Christian rulers did their best to rid themselves of all remaining Muslims within their realm, despite the promises they had sworn to leave them in peace. By the early 17th century the last Muslims had been either driven into exile or forced to convert and Spain was officially a 100 per cent Catholic country. And so things stayed until more tolerant times arrived. No sooner was Franco dead and the transition to democracy in progress than Muslims began to re-establish themselves in Spain, particularly in Granada. The first small communities were of converts to Islam, Spanish nationals who had adopted the faith. Spain's modern Muslims claim (with some justification) that they are not practicants of an alien religion but the heirs to their co-religionists who had lived in Granada for generations before the arrival of the Catholic Monarchs.

geography, ecology and botany. If all this just whets your
appetite you can always stay in a cave yourself (see page 40).
🚌 Bus: 34 leaves from Plaza Nueva every hour.

Abadía del Sacromonte ⓐ Camino del Sacromonte ☎ 958 221
445 🕐 by 45-minute guided tour only at 11.00, 12.00, 13.00, 16.00,
17.00 & 18.00 Tues–Sat, same times Sun but no 12.00 visit.
Admission charge

Centro de Interpretación del Sacromonte ⓐ Barranco de los
Negros ☎ 958 215 120 ⓦ www.sacromontegranada.com
🕐 10.00–14.00, 17.00–21.00 Tues–Sun. Admission charge

CULTURE

Museo Arqueológico

A handsome Renaissance building with Plateresque portal and
magnificent staircase serves as Granada's small but interesting
archaeology museum with exhibits mainly from Roman times
but also from the Iberians and Visigoths.
ⓐ Casa de Castril, Carrera del Darro 43 ☎ 958 225 640
🕐 14.30–20.00 Tues, 09.00–20.30 Wed–Sat, 09.00–14.30 Sun.
Admission charge but free to EU residents

Palacio de Dar Al-Horra

This house between Plaza de San Miguel Bajo and the walls of the
Albaicín was built in the 15th century on the orders of the mother
of Boabdil (the last Nasrid king of Granada). It is down a blind
alleyway and it takes some finding, but it is worth the effort to

◆ Plaza Nueva's Real Chancilleria, built in the 16th century

get a more realistic idea of what buildings must have looked like in Muslim Granada. The Sala de la Reina (Queen's Room) has a beautiful gallery giving views over the back part of the Albaicín.

FLAMENCO

Flamenco is the music, song and dance of Andalucía, particularly of the gypsy community. You can see it and hear it at several places in Granada, particularly in the cave quarter of Sacromonte, which has its own dance variant, the *zambra*. Purists would say you have to be in the right place at the right time for a spontaneous performance of the real thing. Indeed, it is undeniable that most venues (*tablaos*) in Granada are geared up for tourists, but that shouldn't put you off if you enjoy on the level of entertainment rather than sociology. The essence of flamenco is the rough wailing voice of the singer that is often unaccompanied, except by rhythmic clapping. The rapid strumming of a guitar is often added. Songs are never less than full-on passionate and express a range of emotions – mainly sadness and torment. In true flamenco, neither the song nor the dance follows a prescribed script: they are never done the same way twice. The performer continues for as long as his emotions dictate and his stamina will allow. Flamenco is a living music form and several of today's leading exponents are more interested in exploring fusions between flamenco and other genres, such as jazz and rock, rather than clinging to a mythical purity from the past.

At the top of the house is a tower with even better views all round.

🅐 Callejón de las Monjas ☎ no phone 🕙 10.00–14.00 Mon–Fri

RETAIL THERAPY

Alhacaba This ceramics shop near Plaza Larga also sells a few books and maps and usefully serves cold drinks. More prosaically, it has toilets for the use of customers. 🅐 Placeta Almona 2 ☎ 958 205 024 🕙 09.30–13.30, 16.00–20.00

Al Sur de Granada All good, edible things made in the province of Granada are sold in this shop behind the Elvira gateway. Choice items include hams from Trevélez, cheeses (both goats' and sheep's), chestnut preserves and local wines. You are welcome to taste anything before you buy. From 19.30 the shop turns into a bar. As a bonus you can book rural accommodation here and arrange walking and riding excursions. 🅐 Calle Elvira 150 ☎ 958 270 245 🌐 www.alsurdegranada.net 🕙 10.30–15.30, 17.00–24.00 Mon–Sat, open from 12.00 Sun

Calderería Nueva This sloping pedestranised street is like a slice of the East transplanted to Granada, a passageway through an oriental bazaar. It is lined with shops selling Arabic and North African crafts, and by *teterías* (tea shops) with *hookahs* (water pipes) lined up ready to be smoked.

Convento de San Bernardo Sweets are sold by the cloistered nuns of this convent via a turntable, as well as a selection of

wines made in a monastery. ⓐ Convent is on the Carrera del
Darro but the public entrance is round the corner at Gloria 2
ⓣ no phone ⓛ no specific time – when the door is open, go in

TAKING A BREAK

Cafés
Tetería Kasbah £ ❶ One of the largest, oldest and most
inviting *teterías* on the street, the Kasbah serves a range of
teas (some supposedly aphrodisiacal) as well as milkshakes,
juices, wines and spirits and Arabic sweets. On Fridays and
Sundays at 22.00 there is a belly-dancing show and on
Saturdays at the same time there are performances of
flamenco. ⓐ Caldedería Nueva 4 ⓣ 958 227 936

Bars & tapas
Bodegas Castañeda £ ❷ A visit to this classic tapas bar near
Plaza Nueva is almost an essential part of a visit to Granada,
even if it now trades self-consciously on its reputation as a
classic haunt. ⓐ Almireceros 1–3 ⓣ 958 215 464

La Fontana £ ❸ This welcoming bar in an old house with thick
ochre-painted walls and iron-grilled windows manages to
attract two different clienteles. In the afternoon it is a good
place for a quiet coffee but after dark it becomes a hip place to
drink or play pool. ⓐ Puente Cabreras, Carrera del Darro 19
ⓣ 958 227 759 ⓛ 16.00–03.30

El Yunque £ ❹ A tiny bar with tables, set in a charming square with a good list of tapas. There is a dining room for a full meal in an adjacent building. ❸ Plaza de San Miguel Bajo 3
❶ 958 800 090

AFTER DARK

Restaurants
Carmen de Verde Luna £ ❺ Restaurant with a view, and a menu based on fresh seasonal produce. ❸ Camino Nuevo de San Nicolás 16 ❶ 958 291 794

▲ *The pleasant patio of Pilar del Toro*

Pilar del Toro £ ⑥   You can eat tapas in the bar or a full meal in the restaurant, but the really great pleasure here is sitting on the covered patio with a soothingly drizzling fountain in the middle of it. ⓐ Calle Hospital de Santa Ana 12 ⓣ 958 225 470

Colina de Almanzara ££ ⑦   A restored *carmen* serving Moorish-style cuisine. ⓐ Calle Santa Ana 16 ⓣ 958 229 516

Mesón El Trillo £££ ⑧   A restaurant with garden, specialising in Basque cooking. You have to ring the bell to get in. ⓐ Callejón del Aljibe de Trillo 3 ⓣ 958 225 182

Flamenco shows
Sala Albayzin More than just another flamenco venue, this place offers a walking tour of the Albaicín and Sacromonte, and an introduction to flamenco, before the show. ⓐ Carretera de Murcia, Mirador San Cristóbal ⓣ 958 804 646
ⓦ www.flamencoalbaycin.com

Zambra María la Canastera This cave-venue for flamenco shows has been visited by the King of Spain, as well as by film stars such as Anthony Quinn and Ingrid Bergman. Shows begin at 22.30. ⓐ Camino del Sacromonte 89 ⓣ 958 121 183
ⓦ www.granadainfo.com/canastera

◉ *Andalucía's whitewashed houses are a delight*

Day trips from Granada

Granada has plenty to keep you occupied for a few days but it can also be used as a base for excursions to some other interesting places. Top of your list should be Córdoba with its fabulous mosque as a natural complement to a visit to the Alhambra. About the same distance away are the two beautiful Renaissance towns of Úbeda and Baeza. The ancient and monumental Antequera is slightly closer. The other day trip you might want to consider is to the port-city of Málaga, a city that is usually ignored by holidaymakers travelling into and out of its busy airport. It is worth a half-day's visit, especially if you like the work of Pablo Picasso, whose birthplace it is.

GETTING THERE

All the places mentioned in this chapter are reached from Granada by motorway or fast main road and can be visited on a day-trip if you have your own transport, although an overnight stay is preferable. Except for Antequera, which is on the Granada to Algeciras railway line, the best way to get to all of them by public transport is to take a coach (see page 54).

SIGHTS & ATTRACTIONS

Antequera

This ancient town at the crossroads between Seville, Granada, Málaga and Córdoba has two clusters of monuments. One is uphill from the tourist information office through a formal

◯ *Antequera's Arco de los Gigantes*

Granada region

0   18 km
0   12 miles

Madinat Al-Zahra

Córdoba

Córdoba

Andújar

A4

Bujalance

Escañuela

CÓRDOBA

Jaén

A45

Martos

Baena

Santaella

Montilla

Lucena

Priego de Córdoba

Alcalá la Real

Seville

Puente-Genil

A45

A92

A   N   D   A   L

Illora

La Roda

Loja

A92

Granada

Campillos

Antequera

Alhama de Granada

MÁLAGA

Sierra de Almijara

Carratraca

A45

Vélez Málaga

Serranía de Ronda

Málaga

A7

Nerja

Monda

E15

La Herradura

16th-century gateway, the Arco de los Gigantes (Giants' Arch), and includes the Renaissance church of Real Colegiata de Santa María la Mayor and the remains of a Muslim fortress, the Alcazaba.

The other group of sights is on the edge of the town and far older than anything else you will see in Andalucía. The largest of Antequera's three prehistoric constructions (of unknown purpose) is the Dólmen de Menga, dating from 2500 BC, but the most interesting is the Dólmen de Romeral, which has a domed chamber – the first case of intentional architectural construction in Europe.

Tourist information ⓐ Plaza San Sebastían ⓣ 952 708 142
ⓦ www.antequera.es

Dolmens ⓐ On the road out towards Archidona ⓛ 09.00–18.00 Tues–Sat, 09.30–14.30 Sun. Admission charge

Baeza & Úbeda

These two towns stand together on adjacent hills amid the olive groves of Jaén province. The smaller of the two is Baeza, which has an historic centre compact enough to stroll around in half an hour, but worth longer if you have the time. The place to start your tour is the immaculate Plaza del Pópulo just off the main square, the Plaza de la Constitución. Next to it are two gateways: the Puerta de Jaén and the Arco de Villalar. Head uphill from here to reach the cathedral, which looks across a square at a seminary on which students have left graffiti in elegant calligraphy. Downhill again and you come to the Palacio de Jabalquinto, famous for its Isabelline façade. On the other side of Plaza de la Constitución is one other building worth seeing, the Ayuntamiento (town hall), which once served as a prison.

⬥ The church of El Salvador, on Úbeda's main square

The larger town of Úbeda is a museum of Renaissance architecture (once you have penetrated its modern suburbs). Many of its buildings are by the architect Andrés de Vandelvira, working for two nobles in the pay of the King of Spain, Francisco de los Cobos and Juan Vázquez de Molina. Make straight for the Plaza de Vázquez de Molina, at the end of which stands the church of El Salvador, which has elaborate interior decoration. On the north side of the square are the former residence of the Dean of Málaga, which is now a parador hotel (you can step inside to see the patio) and the Palacio de las Cadenas, the town hall. Across the square are the Antiguo Pósito (a granary) and the church of Santa María de los Reales Alcázares. There are few buildings in Úbeda that are not ostentatiously Renaissance, but the finest of them is the Iglesia de San Pablo, built in the 13th century, which has one Gothic and one Romanesque door. Another is the 14th-century Casa Mudéjar, which houses Úbeda's archaeological museum.

Tourist information:
Baeza ⓐ Casa del Pópulo, Plaza del Pópulo ⓣ 953 740 444
Tourist information:
Úbeda ⓐ Baja del Marqués ⓣ 953 755 521 ⓦ www.ubedainteresa.com

Córdoba

Roman Córdoba was the capital of southern Spain and the birthplace of the poet Lucan and the philosopher Seneca. But it was after the Muslim invasion of Spain in the 8th century that it truly came into its own. In 929 Abd al-Rahman III declared himself caliph of Spain, with Córdoba as its capital. In the 10th and 11th centuries, while the rest of Europe was wallowing in a

🔺 *Explore the old Jewish quarter of Córdoba*

cultural dark ages, the civilised place to be was in Muslim Córdoba where Christians and Jews were treated with tolerance, and art and learning thrived.

The magnificence that once existed can today be seen in the famous mosque (*mezquita*) that dominates the city centre and is one of the key sights of Andalucía. It was built on the site of a Visigothic church and is the work of four caliphs. What impresses most is the immense size of the prayer hall whose roof is supported by over 800 two-tier horseshoe arches rising from slender columns – many of which are recycled from Roman and Visigothic buildings. On the southern wall is a *mihrab* (prayer niche) decorated with intricate plasterwork and mosaics. When Córdoba was reconquered by the Christians, they couldn't leave such a structure untouched and in the 16th century a cathedral was dropped incongruously into the middle of it. The old minaret was simultaneously dressed up as a belfry.

For a more down-to-earth idea of medieval Córdoba, take a walk around the Judería, the old Jewish quarter of the city near the mosque. This is a delightful jumble of shady alleyways and whitewashed houses decorated with wrought-iron grilles and flowerpots. Many of them have secretive patios that are opened to the public in a special fiesta in May. Look out for the Sinagoga (synagogue), no more than a delightful square hall with richly decorated walls, one of the only three remaining in Spain.

There is just one drawback to visiting Córdoba: parking. If you are visiting for the day by car the best policy is to head for the underground multistorey car park on Avenida del Aeropuerto (which, as its name says, goes towards the airport), 15 minutes' walk from the monuments.

Outside Córdoba is Madinat Al–Zahra, a city built by caliph Abd al-Rahman III, which only survived 70 years before being ruined in a civil war. It is now the third-largest archaeological dig in Europe (after Pompeii and Knossos) but only a tenth of its ruins have so far been uncovered.

Tourist information ⓐ Caballerizas Reales 1 ⓣ 957 201 774 ⓦ www.turismodecordoba.org

Mezquita ⓐ Cardenal Herrero 1 ⓣ 957 470 512 ⓛ 08.30–19.30 Mon–Sat (closing time sometimes varies), 08.30–10.15, 14.00–19.30 Sun. Admission charge but free between 08.30 and 10.00 on weekdays

Sinagoga ⓐ Judíos ⓣ 957 202 928 ⓛ 09.30–14.00, 15.30–17.30 Tues–Sun. Admission charge but free to EU citizens

Madinat Al-Zahra ⓐ 10 km (6 miles) west of Córdoba off the main road towards Palma del Río ⓣ 957 329 130 ⓦ www. juntadeandalucia.es/cultura/madinatalzahra ⓛ 10.00–18.30 Tues–Sat, 10.00–14.00 Sun. Admission charge but free for EU citizens

Málaga

Málaga's most important monument is the Alcazaba, a Moorish fortress entered through a series of horseshoe arches. Above it on the top of the hill is a castle of more recent construction, the Gibralfaro, which affords great views of the city. (To get to the latter, you might prefer to take the car to the top of the hill.)

Málaga makes great play of being Pablo Picasso's birthplace, even if the artist left when he was only ten years old and made his reputation elsewhere. The Museo Picasso displays a collection of 155 of his lesser works in a restored mansion, which also has some superb 6th-century BC Phoenician ruins in its basement.

Tourist information:
Alcazaba ⓐ Calle Alcazabilla ❶ no phone ⊕ 09.30–20.00 summer; 08.30–19.00 winter. Admission charge
Gibralfaro ⓐ To get there by car follow the signs from Plaza del General Torrijos. ❶ no phone ⊕ 09.00–20.00 (closes 18.00 in winter) Ⓝ Bus 35. Admission charge
Museo Picasso ⓐ Calle San Agustin 8 ❶ 902 443 377
⊕ 10.00–20.00 Tues–Sun (closes 21.00 on Fri & Sat). Admission charge but free on last Sun of month after 15.00

RETAIL THERAPY

Córdoba
Zoco Municipal This pretty courtyard close to the synagogue is occupied by craftsmen and women who can be seen at work in their studios. There's a shop selling their wares as you enter from the street. ⓐ Calle Judíos

TAKING A BREAK

Antequera
Los Dólmenes £ Straightforward place to eat local food. For a starter, try Antequera's typical cold soup, *porra*. ⓐ Cruz El Romeral, next to the roundabout near Romeral Dolmen ❶ 952 845 956

Úbeda
Mesón Navarro £ A reasonably priced and very good menu is served here, but there are also good bar meals, too, for a snack at any time of day. ⓐ Plaza del Ayuntamiento 2 ❶ 953 790 638

AFTER DARK

Restaurants: Córdoba

Bodegas Campos £££ Wine *bodega* transformed into restaurant.
A delightful place in itself but the food is also excellent.
ⓐ Lineros 32 ☎ 957 497 500

El Churrasco £££ The city's classic restaurant dispersed around
several patios and other pleasant dining spaces. Specialises in
grilled meats. ⓐ Romero 16 ☎ 957 290 819

⬥ Málaga's dramatic Muslim fortress, the Alcazaba

Bars & tapas: Córdoba

Taberna San Miguel £ Better known as 'El Pisto', a well-known old bar on a bullfighting theme where tapas are served along with Montilla-Moriles wines (the local equivalent of sherry).
ⓐ Plaza San Miguel 1 ❶ 957 470 166

Flamenco shows: Córdoba

Tablao El Cardenal Puts on a flamenco show Mon–Sat at 22.30.
ⓐ Torrijos 10 ❶ 957 483 112

ACCOMMODATION

Córdoba

Maestre £ A hotel, hostal and set of one- or two-bedroom self-catering apartments close to the mosque, all of which are extremely good value for central Córdoba. Underground parking available. ⓐ Romero Barros 4–6 ❶ 957 472 410
ⓦ www.hotelmaestre.com

Casa de los Naranjos ££ A small hotel with only 20 rooms in the old part of the city. Some of the furnishings were made by local craftsmen. Internet access available. ⓐ Isabel Losa 8 ❶ 957 470 587 ⓦ www.casadelosnaranjos.com

Lola ££–£££ Any hotel that dares to advertise itself as 'the most beautiful hotel in Andalucía' must be worth taking a chance on. Each of the eight rooms is individually furnished with a touch of homeliness. The hotel is situated close to the mosque.
ⓐ Romero 3 ❶ 957 200 305 ⓦ www.hotelconencantolola.com

Granada province

Granada is the capital city of a small province of the same
name, which offers a number of possible excursions. The two
most popular trips are to the Alpujarras, over the other side of
the Sierra Nevada, and down to the coast. Either can be done in
a day but you'll be much less stressed if you take two days or
more, especially if you are travelling by public transport.

GETTING THERE

There are buses to the main towns and cities of the province,
but the only way to see the countryside is by hire car. In winter
you might be most tempted by the slopes of the Sierra Nevada,
which offer skiing within easy reach of the city (see page 35).

SIGHTS & ATTRACTIONS

The Alpujarras & the Sierra Nevada
When the Moors were forced to leave Granada they found
refuge not too far away in the valleys of the Alpujarras. They
were not allowed to live in peace there for long, however, before
being forced to choose between exile and conversion. The only
traces of them today are in the architecture of the villages they
left behind. For centuries life was hard in the Alpujarras and the
people poor, but in recent decades the area has been 'discovered'
by Spaniards and foreigners seeking a simpler life in the country
– most famously the bestselling author Chris Stewart (see box,
page 120).

The countryside of the Alpujarras is good walking and horse-trekking terrain and in spring and early summer is full of wild flowers, including many orchids.

Heading for the Alpujarras from Granada you pass first through Lanjarón – a spa town that distributes Andalucía's most

○ *The lovely hillside villages of Bubión and Capileira*

popular brand of bottled water. The next town on the road is Órgiva, but you don't need to go into it. Instead turn off just outside it onto the main road through the Alpujarras. Climbing up the valley and winding around the contours, this will bring you directly to the Barranco de Poqueira and three pretty villages.

Lowest down, and the first you reach, is Pampaneira. On the higher slopes are Bubión and Capileira. All three are built in the same way: a jumble of white houses with flat gravel roofs, each with an over-tall chimney rising out of it. Their streets are narrow, twisting, tapering and often stepped. Everywhere you look there are delightful details: porticoes, balconies and flowerpots.

Beyond Capileira, the mountains block communications to the north, except for a high-level road across the Sierra Nevada from Capileira to the ski-resort (see page 35) on the other side. From spring to autumn, you can take a minibus excursion up

GERALD BRENAN & CHRIS STEWART

No one much beyond Granada had heard of the poor, backward Alpujarras before an Englishman, Gerald Brenan, installed himself there after fighting in World War I. He wrote about his experiences in a classic travel book, *South from Granada*. Among the visitors to his remote southern hideout were Virginia Woolf and her husband Lytton Strachey (who found that olive oil caused him indigestion and riding a mule played havoc with his piles). Sadly there is nothing to see in Brenan's adoptive village of Yegen except a dull plaque on a wall. Decades later the Alpujarras were back on bookshelves everywhere with the success of *Driving Over Lemons* by sometime Genesis drummer turned sheep-shearer, Chris Stewart. As with many other like-minded people from Spain and abroad, Stewart has chosen to settle in the Alpujarras because of the quality of life it offers and he writes about it with knowledge, humour and affection.

part of this road from the Sierra Nevada National Park's Hoya del Portillo checkpoint above Capileira. This takes you close to La Veleta 3,398 m (11,149 ft) and Mulhacén 3,481 m (11,421 ft). The Sierra Nevada is the second-highest mountain chain in Europe after the Alps and its highest parts have only sparse, hardy vegetation. (You can also get up to the heights of the Sierra Nevada by minibus from the Hoya de la Mora National Park checkpoint above the ski resort, which is much closer to Granada.)

The main road through the Alpujarras continues to wriggle around the mountainsides from the Poqueira valley eastwards and there are more villages to see along the way both on and off it. Two pretty places a short way down the slope are Mecina Fondales and Ferreirola.

By the time you have got to Trevélez, Spain's highest town, at an altitude of 1,476 m (4,840 ft), where hams are cured in the dry mountain air, you've seen the best of the scenery. Your only options are to double back or go on a bit further and make a round trip by taking a right turning south to get back to Órgiva, via the small wine town of Torvizcón. A more arduous route is to cross the Sierra Nevada over its only pass, the Puerto de la Ragua, and pick up the motorway back to Granada from Guadix, but it's a long car journey with lots of curves.

Sierra Nevada National Park minibus tours ☎ 630 959 739

Costa Tropical (Tropical Coast)

Granada province's short shoreline is the most attractive stretch of Spain's southern Mediterranean coast and is only about an hour's drive from the city, making it theoretically possible to

combine a day's sunbathing with a visit to the Alhambra, or even to fit in skiing and swimming in the sea on the same day!

The name 'Tropical Coast' comes from the many fruit orchards that extend up the valleys behind the coastal towns. A prevailing frost-free microclimate allows farmers to produce avocados, mangoes, custard apples (*chirimoyas*) and other exotic fruits – all of which you will see on sale at stalls by the roadside.

The coast's largest town is Motril, once centre of a sugar-cane refining industry, but it is not of much interest to the

THE SIGH OF THE MOOR

The last, hapless Muslim king of Granada, Muhammad XI, universally known as Boabdil, didn't have much choice in the end but to hand over the city he loved to the Catholic Monarchs on the best terms of surrender he could manage. It was only a matter of time before the Christians moved in, but at least the capitulations he signed in the nearby town of Santa Fe left him with a shred of dignity. The victors entered Granada on 2 January 1492 while Boabdil and his entourage left by the back door, going into exile in the nearby Alpujarras. A much-repeated story has it that Boabdil was heading south across the last low pass from which it was possible to see the city and he began to cry. His mother admonished him with the words, 'That's right: cry like a child over that which you couldn't defend as a man.' The pass, on the motorway towards the coast, has been known ever since as the Suspiro del Moro, or the Moor's Sigh.

casual visitor. A few headlands round to the west is the large resort of Almuñecar, which is believed to have been founded by the Phoenicians and is now overrun by foreign tourists. The best beach on the coast is that of La Herradura (between Almuñécar and Nerja), which is a famously good place for scuba diving (you can take a trial plunge with the dive school at Marina del Este).

The prettiest place on the Tropical Coast, however, is Salobreña, a compact mass of white houses clambering over a great rock set back from the sea. Climb the maze of steep

○ *Salobreña and its impressive Arab castle perched on the hill*

streets, steps and narrow alleys and you will reach a well-preserved Arab castle from which there are great views.

Guadix

Across the pass of Puerto de la Mora (1,390 m/4,560 ft) from Granada, heading east on the motorway towards Murcia and Almería, you descend into an ancient lake bed in which stands the curious town of Guadix. This has a group of handsome monuments in the centre but no one comes to see them. What holds most fascination is the Barriada de las Cuevas, a suburb of mudhills drilled with innumerable cave homes – a much larger troglodyte community than Granada's Sacromonte. About 3,000 people live underground here, some in surprising luxury, and caves are sought after and traded just as houses and flats

⬤ *Cool and comfortable cave homes in Guadix*

would be elsewhere. Several caves have been turned into cosy and comfortable hotels.

RETAIL THERAPY

Albayalde If the splendour of the Alhambra's decoration has left you feeling you'd like to make some improvements at home, you can always order a set of reproduction Moorish tiles at this shop outside Órgiva. ⓐ Cortijo del Cura, Órgiva, Alpujarras (near Hotel Taray) ⓣ 958 785 199 ⓦ www.albayalde.eu

TAKING A BREAK

El Chambao de Joaquín ££ It looks like a mere hut near the end of La Herradura beach, but this is a cunningly sophisticated place that may cater largely for foreign tourists but is still a great place to eat fish and seafood. At weekends, giant paellas are prepared. ⓐ La Herradura beach ⓣ 958 640 044

El Peñon ££ Head for Salobreña beach and you won't be able to miss this restaurant that is affixed to the side of a rock, with a delightful shaded terrace over the water. The fish and seafood couldn't be fresher and you can often watch it being grilled on spits in the traditional way over an open fire. ⓐ Playa del Peñón, Salobreña ⓣ 958 610 538

AFTER DARK

Teide £ Good salads and local food in this restaurant in the Barranco de Poqueira. ⓐ Carretera, Bubión ⓣ 958 763 084

Mesón Poqueira ££ A good place to sample Alpujarreño cooking.
ⓐ Doctor Castilla 5, Capileira ⓣ 958 763 048

ACCOMMODATION

Alcazaba de Busquistar ££ You'd be forgiven for thinking that
this was another Alpujarran village because it has been built to
create that illusion, even with its own church tower. Most rooms
have a fireplace or wood-burning stove. ⓐ on the road from
Trevélez towards Ugíjar ⓣ 958 858 687
ⓦ www.alcazabadelbusquistar.com

Almuñécar Playa ££ A large chain hotel that, as its name states,
is right on Almuñécar beach and perfectly placed for exploring
the town. There is a buffet restaurant and a swimming pool.
ⓐ Paseo San Cristóbal ⓣ 958 639 450 ⓦ www.playasenator.com

Taray ££ This 'hacienda-style' hotel could serve as a base for
visiting both the Alpujarras and Granada. It's also a good place
if you just want to have lunch in relaxing surroundings. The
gardens are planted with orange, lemon and pomegranate trees
and there are tanks of trout on site to supply the restaurant
menu. ⓐ on the road out of Órgiva going towards Torvizcón
ⓣ 958 784 525 ⓦ www.hoteltaray.com

ⓞ *A Granada post box*

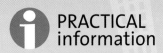

EXTRANJERO

Directory

GETTING THERE

By air

Granada airport receives mainly domestic flights but it does receive a few international flights, notably those operated by Iberia, Spain's national carrier and the budget airline Ryanair. Málaga airport offers much more choice. Flying time from Britain is around two and a half hours. For details of getting from the airport to the city centre see page 50.

Iberia Flights from the UK, most European and many other major airports. It, or its subsidiaries, operates domestic flights within Spain. ⓣ 902 400 500; in UK 0870 609 050; office in Granada 958 245 200 ⓦ www.iberia.com

Ryanair ⓣ 958 181 320; in UK 0871 246 0000 ⓦ www.ryanair.com

Many people are aware that air travel emits CO_2, which contributes to climate change. You may be interested in the possibility of lessening the environmental impact of your flight through the charity Climate Care, which offsets your CO_2 by funding environmental projects around the world. Visit ⓦ www.climatecare.org

By train

Mainline and local trains are operated by the national company RENFE (Red Nacional de Ferrocarriles Españoles). Full details of services can be obtained from ⓣ 902 240 202 ⓦ www.renfe.es. Andalucía has a patchy railway network. The train is a convenient way to get to Granada from Madrid, Seville, Almería and Algeciras, but not from Córdoba and Málaga. The journey time

from Madrid is about five hours. To plan a rail trip from the UK to Spain, it's best to go through an international agent such as Rail Europe ❸ 178 Piccadilly, London W1 (nearest tube Piccadilly Circus or Green Park) ❶ 08708 371 371 ⓦ www.raileurope.co.uk. It takes about two days non-stop to get to Granada from London by rail.

By road

From any of the French Channel ports, head south to Biarritz and cross the frontier at the western end of the Pyrenees (between Hendaye and Irún) to reach San Sebastian. Turn inland for Vitoria-Gasteiz and pick up the N1 motorway for Madrid at Burgos. Madrid's orbital motorways take some navigating. The best policy is to go around Madrid to the east on the M40 following signs first for Zaragoza (but don't turn off for that city), then Valencia, then Córdoba. If you're lucky you'll find yourself heading due south on the NIV motorway through La Mancha (past Aranjuez) and eventually through the spectacular pass of Despeñaperros into Andalucía. At Bailén turn off onto the N323 motorway which skirts past Jaén to reach Granada.

Alternatively, to save driving through France, take a ferry from Portsmouth to Bilbao or Plymouth to Santander (crossing 24–30 hours) and drive south to Burgos and thence to Madrid.

Driving around the centre of Granada may take some getting used to and is best avoided in favour of walking and public transport. Parking can be both difficult and expensive and some people choose to double-park, which makes the traffic problem worse.

Spain drives on the right and its highway code is similar to that of other European countries, with internationally recognisable traffic signs. The police can issue on-the-spot fines for traffic offences and being a foreigner does not give you exemption. Seatbelts are obligatory and children under 12 should travel in the back. Speed limits are 120 km/h (74 mph) on motorways, 100 km/h (62 mph) on roads and 50 km/h (31 mph) in built-up areas. It is forbidden to drive under the influence of alcohol. Most national driving licences are valid but it is advisable to have an International Driving Permit. In your car you must carry a red warning triangle, replacement light bulbs and a reflective jacket in the passenger compartment to wear in case of roadside emergency. Petrol (*gasolina*) is available as *super*, *normal* (both leaded), *sin plomo* (unleaded) and *gasoil* (diesel).

Car hire

When hiring a car you will be asked to show your passport and an EU or International Driving Permit. All the major car hire companies have offices in Granada and rates are competitive, but you can usually get the best deal by reserving a car from home at the same time as making a flight booking.

Avis ⓣ 902 135 531 Ⓦ www.avis.es

Hertz ⓣ 902 402 405 Ⓦ www.hertz.es

ENTRY FORMALITIES

Most visitors, including citizens of all EU countries, the US, Canada, Australia and New Zealand, require only a valid passport to enter Spain. Visitors from South Africa must have a visa. There is no restriction on what items you may bring in with you as a tourist but you'll find almost everything you need locally. In Spain you are obliged by law to carry your passport with you at all times, in case the police ask for identification.

MONEY

The Spanish currency is the euro. It is divided into 100 cents. There are coins of 1 and 2 euros and of 1, 2, 5, 10, 20 and 50 cents. The notes are of 5, 10, 20, 50 and 100 euros.

Banks are generally open only in the morning from 09.00–13.30 Monday to Friday but there are many cash machines in Granada where you can get money out with a debit/credit card. Credit cards are accepted for payment almost everywhere except in smaller bars, shops and *pensiones*. Traveller's cheques can be cashed in banks and big hotels. Personal cheques are not accepted anywhere.

TRAVEL INSURANCE

Although EU citizenship gives you basic health cover in Spain it is advisable to take out personal travel insurance as well. This can be obtained from your travel agent, airline operator or any insurance company. Make sure it gives adequate cover not only for medical expenses but also for loss or theft of possessions, personal liability and repatriation in an emergency. If you are going to Spain by car ask your insurer for a green card and check with them on the cover you will need for damage, loss or theft of the vehicle and for legal costs in the event of an accident. If you hire a car you will be asked whether you want to pay extra for collision insurance. You may already be covered for this by your normal UK car insurance.

HEALTH, SAFETY & CRIME

British citizens – as all EU nationals – are entitled to free treatment from the Spanish social security system on production of a European Health Insurance Card (EHIC). Many travellers prefer to take out private medical insurance before travelling to Spain to give them greater choice of healthcare, should the worst happen. Like any European city, Granada has its share of petty crime but most of it is opportunist and a few simple precautions will make sure you are not an easy target. Watch out for pickpockets in crowded places like markets and bars and keep your bag across your chest and in front of you. Leave valuables in a hotel safe and never leave anything on display in a parked car.

OPENING HOURS

Shops Usual opening hours are 09.00 or 10.00–13.30, 17.00–20.30 Mon–Sat. In the summer some shops open later in the afternoon, when the heat starts to die down, and stay open correspondingly later.

Department stores and other large shops open continuously from 10.00–21.00. Shops are generally closed on Sundays except on special occasions such as the run-up to Christmas.

Post offices generally open 08.30–14.30 Mon–Fri, 09.30–13.00 Sat. The main post office has longer opening hours (see page 134).

Banks usually open 09.00–13.30.

Offices (government and private business) Open 09.00–14.00, 16.00–20.00 Mon–Fri. In summer, many offices work a reduced day from 08.00–15.00 and then close until the next morning.

Museums generally open 09.00–13.00, 16.00–20.00 Tues–Sat and perhaps Sun morning. They usually close on Mondays, although there are exceptions.

Restaurants Mealtimes in Spain are later than in the rest of Europe. Breakfast in hotels is served 07.30–10.00. Lunch is 14.00–16.00 and dinner generally 21.00–23.00.

Entertainment Larger cinemas have several showings a day between 16.00 and 23.00. Some theatres offer two daily performances at 18.00 and 22.00. Bars for drinking and musical venues open 21.00–03.00 and discos from 11.30–05.00 or 06.00.

TOILETS

Granada has few public toilets and the most convenient thing to do is go into a bar or café – in which case it is polite to buy a drink. Another option is to use those in a department store like El Corte Inglés. There are several words for toilets in Spanish, the most common being *servicios*, *aseos* and *lavabos*.

🔺 *Even Granada's toilets have the Moorish touch*

CHILDREN

In Spain, children simply fit into ordinary life. There may not be many special facilities for them but this lack is more than made up for by a general tolerance and willingness to help. There are few attractions specifically for children in Granada and you might be best to spend a day or two in the city and then head for the beach. One particularly child-friendly place is the **Parque de las Ciencias**, a sophisticated science museum with ten indoor galleries using the latest technology for its interactive exhibits and a large outdoor area, which includes a maze, butterfly house, olive oil mill and planetarium. ⓐ Avenida del Mediterráneo ① 958 131 900 ⓦ www.parqueciencias.com ⓛ 10.00–19.00 Tues–Sat, 10.00–15.00 Sun. Admission charge

COMMUNICATIONS

Telephones

Local, national and international calls can be made from public phone booths (*cabinas*) in the street. They operate with coins or cards. Instructions are written in several languages. Some call boxes take credit cards. Phone cards (*tarjetas telefónicas*) are on sale at tobacconists (*estancos*) and post offices.

You can also phone from *locutorios*, public telephone centres, which are quieter; pay at the counter when you have finished your call. Calls from a hotel room are more expensive than from phone boxes or *locutorios*.

Post

The main post office is on Puerta Real. It is open from 08.30 to 20.30 Monday to Friday and 09.30 to 14.00 on Saturdays. If you

just want stamps you can buy them at tobacconists (*estancos*).
To send a card or a letter up to 20 g to a country within the EU
currently costs 0.57 euros and 0.78 euros to the rest of the
world. After that, prices vary according to weight. Postboxes are
yellow. To send a telegram ☎ 902 197 197.

Internet

There are internet cafés (*cafés cibernéticos*) all over the city.
The largest and most centrally located is:

Navegaweb @ Calle de los Reyes Católicos 55 ☎ 958 210 528

DIALLING CODES

To make an international call dial **00** + the country code
+ the phone number omitting the initial zero. Spain's
country code is **34**. Granada's provincial area code,
958, must be dialled before all phone numbers, even for
local calls.

The country code for the UK is **44**, for Ireland **353**, for the
US and Canada **1**, for Australia **61**, for New Zealand **64** and
for South Africa **27**.

For international information ☎ **11825**

For national information ☎ **11818**

You can also find phone numbers at
🌐 www.paginasamarillas.es (yellow pages) and
🌐 www.paginasamarillas.es www.paginasblancas.es
(the normal phone book listing subscribers).

For any other information see the website of the national
phone company, Telefónica 🌐 www.telefonica.es

Also handy for the city centre is:

Uninet ⓐ Plaza de la Encarnación 2 ❶ 958 208 382 ⓦ www.uninet.us

Media

The most popular European and US newspapers, including *International Herald Tribune*, *Financial Times* and *Guardian Europe*, are available from news stands (*kioskos de prensa*) in the centre of the city as well as at the airport. Many hotel rooms have satellite TV with programmes in English.

ELECTRICITY

Spain's electricity supply is 220 V, but you may find an anachronistic 125-V outlet occasionally in an older building, and for sensitive appliances like computers and mobile phones it is worth double-checking the voltage before plugging them in. All plugs in Spain have two round pins so electrical devices from the UK will only work with an adaptor. Visitors from North America require a transformer.

TRAVELLERS WITH DISABILITIES

Spain hasn't got many facilities for travellers with disabilities but the situation is slowly changing. More information is available from **COCEMFE** ⓐ Luis Cabrera 63, Madrid ❶ 917 443 600 ⓦ www.cocemfe.es **RADAR** (Royal Association for Disability and Rehabilitation) at ❶ 020 7250 3222 ⓦ www.radar.org.uk and **Holiday Care Service** at ❶ 0845 124 9971 ⓦ www.holidaycare.org.uk offer some information for disabled people visiting Spain.

TOURIST INFORMATION

Before travelling you can obtain general information from the
Spanish Tourist Office by making a prior appointment.
ⓐ 79 New Cavendish Street, London W1W 6XB ① 020 7486 8077
ⓦ www.spain.info
For information about Andalucía in particular see
ⓦ www.andalucia.org. Another useful site, not official, is
ⓦ www.andalucia.com

The main tourist office in Granada is the **Centro Municipal de
Recepción Turística** ⓐ Calle Virgen Blanca 9 ① 902 405 045
ⓦ www.granadatur.com but perhaps the most useful tourist
information office is the one just off the top end of Plaza Nueva
ⓐ Santa Ana 4 ① 958 225 990. There are also information points
at Puerta Real, in the Alhambra and in Plaza Bib-Rambla. For
information about visiting Granada province there is a separate
tourist office ⓐ Plaza Mariana Pineda 10 ① 958 247 128
ⓦ www.turismodegranada.org

BACKGROUND READING

Required reading for visiting Granada is *Tales of the Alhambra*
by Washington Irving (see page 64). *South From Granada* by
Gerald Brenan is another classic. The more recent *Driving Over
Lemons* by Chris Stewart is a good introduction to the
Alpujarras.

Emergencies

EMERGENCY NUMBERS

If you remember only one emergency number make it 112 which will get you through to an operator whose job it is to put you through to the service you need. Emergency numbers are listed in telephone directories under *Servicios de Urgencias*.

General Emergencies 112   **Fire Brigade** 080
Policía Nacional 091   **Policía Municipal** 092

Police

Spain effectively has three police forces. The Policía Municipal is responsible for traffic problems and low-level policing. The Policía Nacional is in charge of more serious crime. The paramilitary Guardia Civil, meanwhile, takes care of highway patrols and customs. You can turn to any of them in the event of an emergency.

Embassies & consulates

Australia ⓐ Federico Rubio 14, Seville ⓣ 954 220 971
ⓦ www.embaustralia.es
Canada ⓐ Plaza Malagueta 3, Málaga ⓣ 952 22 33 46
ⓦ www.canada-es.org
Ireland ⓐ Plaza de Santa Cruz 6, Seville ⓣ 954 216 361
New Zealand ⓐ 3rd floor, Plaza de la Lealtad 2, Madrid
ⓣ 915 230 226
South Africa ⓐ Claudio Coello 91, Madrid ⓣ 914 363 780
UK ⓐ Urb Aljamar, block 7, no 145, Seville ⓣ 954 155 018
ⓦ www.ukinspain.com
US ⓐ Plaza Nueva 8, Seville ⓣ 954 218 571 ⓦ www.embusa.es

MEDICAL SERVICES
Pharmacies

Minor health problems can often be cleared up by consulting a *farmacia*, a chemist's shop, which is indicated by a green cross sign. Pharmacists are trained to advise on common ailments. Out of hours, there is always a *farmacia de guardia* open in every neighbourhood; you'll find its address posted in the window of other *farmacias*. *Farmacias* should not be confused with *parafarmacias*, which sell non-prescription medical supplies and where the staff are not always qualified to give advice.

Ambulances & hospitals

To summon an ambulance, dial **112**.

If you decide to make straight for a hospital, the two closest to the centre are:

Hospital San Juan de Dios ⓐ San Juan de Dios 15 ☎ 958 022 904

Hospital Clínico Universitario San Cecilio ⓐ Avda Doctor Oloriz 16 ☎ 958 023 259

EMERGENCY PHRASES	
Help!	*¡Socorro!*
Stop!	*¡Pare!*
Call a doctor!	*¡Llame a un médico!*
Call an ambulance!	*¡Llame a una ambulancia!*
Call the police!	*¡Llame a la policía!*
Call the fire brigade!	*¡Llame a los bomberos!*
Where is the nearest phone?	*¿Dónde está el teléfono más próximo?*

The publishers would like to thank the following individuals
and organisations for supplying the copyright photographs
for this book:
Nick Inman: all photographs except
Pictures Colour Library: pages 9, 19, 34, 70, 81, 85, 115, 123
World Pictures: pages 7, 45, 61, 105, 111

Copy editor: Jenni Rainford
Proofreader: Ian Faulkner

Send your thoughts to
books@thomascook.com

- **Found a great bar, club, shop or must-see sight that we don't feature?**

- **Like to tip us off about any information that needs updating?**

- **Want to tell us what you love about this handy little guidebook and more importantly how we can make it even handier?**

Then here's your chance to tell all! Send us ideas, discoveries and recommendations today and then look out for your valuable input in the next edition of this title. As an extra 'thank you' from Thomas Cook Publishing, you'll be automatically entered into our exciting prize draw.

Send an email to the above address (stating the book's title) or write to: CitySpots Project Editor, Thomas Cook Publishing, PO Box 227, The Thomas Cook Business Park, Unit 18, Coningsby Road, Peterborough PE3 8SB, UK.